THE
INNER
CIRCLE

"Rick Hawkins illustrates not only the importance but the necessity of healthy relationships. He empowers you to strengthen your inner circle and become a true companion to the people in your life. We all have many relationships to cultivate, and this is the book that will foster that growth."

—John Bevere

"A powerful new work for the Kingdom! In *The Inner Circle*, Pastor Rick Hawkins has masterfully captured the beauty and the power of associations. He illustrates lessons learned that can be applied to personal, professional, family, and ministry relationships. An easy read, you will learn how to discern those around you and to apply wisdom in determining whom you should allow into your inner circle."

—Paula White

THE
INNER
CIRCLE

The VALUE *of* FRIENDSHIP,
TRUST, *and* INFLUENCE

RICK HAWKINS

Published by HonorNet
PO Box 910
Sapulpa, OK 74067
Web site: honornet.net

DEDICATION

The experiences and words in this book are dedicated to those in my inner circle, the center of which is my best friend and wife, Robin.

To the rest—you know who you are—this book is a testimony to the battles we have fought, the walls we have built, and the caves we have shared. We have seen victory snatched from the certainty of defeat, and we have sipped from the cup of friendship that is reserved only for those who stand and face the waning sun setting on the battlefields of life. Our bond has been forged in the heat of the moment, when warriors lose all sense of the conciseness of their surroundings, except for the band of brothers that are *next to* them. Our circle is small, our trust reserved, and our influence multiplied for the purpose of building God's kingdom.

May the banner under which we fight always fly equally high in the haze of war and in the solitude of peace. May its colors never fade and always be clear for all the world to see. May its holes and tears be a testimony of our love and covenant with each other even when we fall and fail. And most of all, when our King of kings and Lord of lords arrives on His white horse of victory, wearing His royal robe dipped in blood to deliver the death blow to our enemy, may our banner be the colors chosen as His praetorian guard. For we are members of *The Inner Circle*, and we value friendship, trust, and influence.

—*Rick Hawkins*

CONTENTS

FOREWORD

It is my pleasure to recommend to you Rick Hawkins as a man of God, as a man of integrity, and as someone who has placed his experiences into words to inspire all who are on the journey to their divine destiny.

Each of us has an inner circle of friends we can trust and with whom we have great influence. A person without an inner circle is emotionally and spiritually defenseless. False friends are like a shadow, keeping close to us while we walk in the sunshine, but leaving us immediately when we cross into the darkness.

The person who has a handful of true friends is wealthy beyond measure. There is unspeakable joy when you can bare your soul to another person without having to weigh thoughts or measure words, but spill them out just as they are—chaff and grain together—certain that a faithful hand will keep what is worth keeping and with a breath of kindness blow the chaff away.

Welcome to the *Inner Circle, The Value of Friendship, Trust, and Influence* by Rick Hawkins.

—John Hagee

Acknowledgments

To my Lord and Savior, Jesus Christ, the creator of my inner circle. May all that I do and say bring glory, honor, and praise to Your name.

A special thanks to my beautiful wife, Robin, my closest confidant and center of my circle, who has supported, inspired, and poured into me with her love, faithfulness, and friendship.

To my grown children, Dustin and Crystal, and their beautiful families, and to my lovely daughter, Kendra, who keeps us smiling and young with her love of life.

To the church that God has blessed me with, Family Praise Center. I am honored and humbled to serve as your shepherd and to count you as part of my circle. I know that I pastor the best church in the world.

Be courteous to all, but intimate with
few; and let those few be well tried
before you give them your confidence.

–General George Washington

We are like chameleons; we take our
hue and the color of our moral
character, from those who are around us.

—John Locke

Chapter One

The Power of Next—Influence

RITISH NATURALIST AND EVANGELIST HENRY Drummond, in his book, *The Greatest Thing in the World*, wrote with convincing clarity about the law of influence and its effects on the human race. "It is the Law of Influence that we become like those whom we habitually admire…. Through all the range of literature, of history, and biography this law presides. Men are all mosaics of other men."[1] No man is an island. We are all influenced by the impact that people *next to* us have had on our lives, for good or for evil. Those who have been abused, ridiculed, scorned, or rejected bear the wounds of those pains in the lining of their soul. On the other hand, those who have been surrounded with acceptance and love and strength have profited by the influence of such positive people in their lives.

Drummond goes on to say that the whole vast pyramid of humanity is built upon this truth. The people around us will leave a deep impact upon us, so choose wisely your friends.

"A few raw, unspiritual, uninspiring men, were admitted to the inner circle of His [Christ's] friendship. The change began at once. Day by day we can almost see the first disciples grow. First there steals over them the faintest possible adumbration of His character, and occasionally, very occasionally, they do a thing or say a thing that they could not have done or said had they not been living there. Slowly the spell of His Life deepens. Reach after reach of their nature is overtaken, thawed, subjugated, sanctified. Their manners soften, their words become more gentle, their conduct more unselfish. As swallows who have found a summer, as frozen buds the spring, their starved humanity bursts into a fuller life. They do not know how it is, but they are different men."[2]

WHO'S STANDING *NEXT TO* YOU?

The person *next to* you will make an indelible mark upon your soul. This is why we must be careful to evaluate the people who stand *next to* us. Our evaluation of these people should not be based upon the world's criterion. Sometimes what appears to be the right folk turn out to be the wrong folk, and often what appears to others to be the wrong folk turn out to be the right folk. Jesus allowed a band of ruffians into His life, avoiding all those highly influential religious leaders that others might have chosen—a strange choice of friends upon which to build His church. Be careful about the standards you set for those who will enter into the secret places of your life. The religiously right might just end up being the woefully wrong.

Those who have served in the military throughout the ages have understood the principle of the "power of next." When the decisions of those around you often determine whether you live or die, a bond like no other is created. In 1993 an elite group of American Rangers and Delta Force soldiers were sent into war-torn Somalia. Their mission was to capture a warlord whose power-hungry regime had cost the country hundreds of thousands of lives. Saddled with faulty local intelligence, and unfamiliar with the backstreets of Mogadishu, the elite force found themselves in a war they didn't understand and in a battle they could not win. I remember watching the news as the rebels dragged the body of an American solider through the streets. The 2001 Academy Award-winning movie, *Black Hawk Down*, was based on the bravery, camaraderie, and terrible events gone wrong during this mission. At the end of the movie after the loss of many comrades, a young Ranger asks a veteran Delta Force cohort why he was preparing to go back into the death trap the backstreets of Mogadishu had become. His response: "There are still men out there. When I go home, people ask me, 'Hey Hoot, why do you do it man, why? Are you some kind of war junkie?' I won't say a …word. Why? They won't understand. They won't understand why we do it. They won't understand it's about the men *next* to you. That's it. That's all it is."[3]

Those who you allow into your inner circle must be companions of trust, honor, duty, integrity, and courage. You must know they are with you in war and peace. We all are developed and shaped in part by the warriors we allow to fight by our side.

Solomon learned this truth from his father and had it right when he said that *he who walks with the wise grows wise, but a companion of fools suffers harm* (Proverbs 13:20). Your closest friends—the ones who speak into your life, the ones who you allow to enter into the inner chamber of your heart—these must be the kind of people who will cover your back and contribute positively to your life.

DEATH OF A NATION

The Jewish nation had forsaken their God, and even though the prophets of God gave one warning after another, they did not change their ways. Sin brings its own evil reward, and for the Jews, danger was just around the corner. "The young brilliant new king of Babylon, Nebuchadnezzar, went out and defeated the Egyptians at Carchemish. He marched on to Judah, during Jehoiakim's reign, and took thousands of Hebrews back to Babylon (including Daniel, who became one of the greatest prophets). Nebuchadnezzar made two more attacks when he heard of the rebellion in Judah. Each time he took captives (including Ezekiel the prophet). King Nebuchadnezzar set up a puppet king (Zedekiah) of David's line to sit on the throne of Judah and made him swear an oath of allegiance (2 Chr 36:10-12).

"Zedekiah was as faithless as the rest of the evil kings of Judah. He then rebelled and allied with other enemies. When Nebuchadnezzar heard he came back for the last time (586 BC) to reduce Jerusalem to rubble and send the Temple up in flames. Zedekiah was forced to witness the slaughter of his sons, then his eyes were put out, and he himself was carried off to Babylon. The Kingdom was over and the 'times of the gentiles' had begun."[4]

> In the eighth year of the reign of the king of Babylon, he took Jehoiachin prisoner. As the Lord had declared, Nebuchadnezzar removed all the

*treasures from the temple of the Lord and from the
royal palace, and took away all the gold articles that
Solomon king of Israel had made for the temple of
the Lord. He carried into exile all Jerusalem: all the
officers and fighting men, and all the craftsmen and
artisans - a total of ten thousand. Only the poorest
people of the land were left.*

—2 Kings 24:12b–14

COLLAPSING OF TIME

After the Babylonian empire fell to the Persians, God would
make His move to fulfill the prophetic word and restore the
beloved city. The Jews had carved out a life for themselves in the
land of Babylon and many would not return. But there was a
remnant of people who still longed to return home, and during
the time of Cyrus that dream would become a reality. When
Cyrus became a king, the first thing that he did was open the
door for the exiled Jews to return.

Zerubbabel was the original contractor called to rebuild
Jerusalem, and Ezra was a worthy associate. Under Zerubbabel,
more than 42,000 Jews returned with plans to rebuild the
foundations of Jerusalem. The prophet Ezra joined him in
commencing the reconstruction of the temple. Because of
Ezra's passion for the Word of the Lord, a spiritual fervor
ignited among the Jews. From the time of Zerubbabel and Ezra
to the time of Nehemiah there was a period of ninety years of
construction.

Then Nehemiah received the mandate as well as the mantle
to go and rebuild the city walls and establish the city gates.
What took ninety years for Ezra and Zerubbabel to accomplish

would only take Nehemiah fifty-two days to complete. In order to quickly complete the work, God collapsed time.

Today we live in a time when God is causing time to collapse as well. What used to take a month is about to take a week. And what used to take a week is about to happen in a day. And what used to take a day is about to take an hour. And what used to take an hour is about to take a moment. Because a moment is all God needs to bring about His purposes. *With only a moment of your time, God can create a momentum in your life that will cause eternal and perpetual change.*

I believe that we are living in the bottleneck of time. Everything is accelerating as time races toward its final conclusion, the manifestation of God's glory, and the fulfillment of His purposes. Just as there have been unbelievable technological advances in this generation, so also in the Spirit there is a great disintegrating of time. The sower is overtaking the reaper. As God worked with Nehemiah in his day, so He is working with us, collapsing time so that we can accomplish more things for His glory at a quicker pace.

How could such an amazing feat as rebuilding Jerusalem happen in such a short time? The first thing we learn here is that when history makes a paradigm shift, it always begins with a person who carries a burden and has caught a vision. No one can deny the power of one life set ablaze by the power of vision and purpose and the potential impact of that life upon society. Nehemiah was that person. Under the sway of heaven's influence, he would carry that heavenly burden and transfer his vision to others.

This is the second thing we learn from history. No one man can accomplish great things by himself. It will take other people who have been influenced by the passion of the one *next to* them. God's anointing resting on Nehemiah was for a very specific purpose so that he could accomplish a very specific objective. He was able to operate on an accelerated timetable because God had called him to that task and given him the perception and power he needed to accomplish it.

But Nehemiah knew he could not do it alone. He needed a team—the right team operating in his or her unique set of gifts—and with this team the work of God could be accomplished in record time.

ONE FOR ALL AND ALL FOR ONE

Knowing how to work with and alongside others for the good of the common cause is one of the great keys to all success. Andrew Carnegie said it best when he said, "Teamwork is the ability to work together toward a common vision. The ability to direct individual accomplishments toward organizational objectives. It is the fuel that allows common people to attain uncommon results."[5] If we cannot work together then we are doomed to fail individually.

Success is dependent upon the ability to work with others. It is also dependent upon who I choose to work alongside. If I choose the right people then I will maximize my opportunity for fulfilling the ultimate dream. Coming together, sharing together, working together, succeeding together—this is God's way of accomplishing His purposes. It is why He puts us in community. On one occasion, Thomas Edison was asked why he had a team of twenty-one assistants, and he replied that if he could solve all the problems himself, he would. In order to fulfill the vision, God knew that Nehemiah would need a team.

The secret of the Church is in her unity, and this is why Jesus prayed for His disciples that they might be one. Corporate victory based upon individual success is a force that cannot be resisted. In the power of the "many made one," Jesus knew that He could accomplish His purposes.

NEXT TO—EXTENDING A HAND TO OTHERS

Before Nehemiah could put the team together, he had to take a good look at the problem. So one night he went out to the streets and walked through the city, and he was able to see the problems quite clearly—burning gates, broken walls, and busted cisterns. Rather than being overwhelmed by the immensity of the task, Nehemiah opened his spirit to God for a heavenly download of vision and purpose. God put into his mind what He wanted to do. Now that the goal was clear, it was time to assemble the team that would be able to accomplish this heavenly plan.

Let's take a look at Nehemiah 3 and observe how he put the power of *next* and *after* to work for him and how he built his team.

> *Then Eliashib the high priest rose up with his brethren the priests, and they builded the sheep gate; they sanctified it, and set up the doors of it; even unto the tower of Meah they sanctified it, unto the tower of Hananeel. And next unto him builded the men of Jericho. And next to them builded Zaccur the son of Imri. But the fish gate did the sons of Hassenaah build, who also laid the beams thereof, and set up the doors thereof, the locks thereof, and the bars thereof. And next unto them repaired Meremoth the son of Urijah, the son of Koz. And next unto them repaired Meshullam the son of*

Berechiah, the son of Meshezabeel. And next unto them repaired Zadok the son of Baana. And next unto them the Tekoites repaired; but their nobles put not their necks to the work of their Lord.
—Nehemiah 3:1-5, KJV

The word *next* appears repeatedly in the book of Nehemiah! The English dictionary tells us that *next* means "adjacent and near; to be adjacent to you; to be near to you; to be close to you." It does not mean to be behind you. It means "to be *next to*, to be closer, to be near; to be adjacent to you." But in the Hebrew language, we see two words that are used for next—*al* and *yad*. *Al* is a prefix that means "upon, above and over." *Yad* means "an open hand for the purpose of means, direction, resources, and power."

These men were standing together in confidence and courage because each one knew that if he should fall, the person next to him would extend his hand toward him, lifting him up so he could continue the work. All of these men were committed to the same goal—the restoration of Jerusalem—and by working together and *next to* each other, the power to reach the goal was greater than any power they might have experienced on their own. The one *next to* us is the one who can lend a helping hand.

The synergistic and simultaneous actions of separate individuals when united together will have a greater total effect than the sum of their individual efforts. In order to create perfect synergy, we must understand the processes of God. Embedded into the plans and purposes of God there is a process by which He will accomplish His purposes. The process is locked up in sequence, series, and succession. Synergy is the harmony created by sequence, series, and succession.

AFTER—SEQUENCE, SERIES, AND SUCCESSION

> *After him repaired Nehemiah the son of Azbuk, the*
> *ruler of the half part of Bethzur, unto the place over*
> *against the sepulchres of David, and to the pool that*
> *was made, and unto the house of the mighty. After*
> *him repaired the Levites, Rehum the son of Bani.*
> *Next unto him repaired Hashabiah, the ruler of the*
> *half part of Keilah, in his part. After him repaired*
> *their brethren, Bavai the son of Henadad, the ruler*
> *of the half part of Keilah.*
> —Nehemiah 3:16-18, KJV

Numerous times we see the use of the word *after* in this passage. God operates in the rhythm of sequence, series, and succession. A *series* is a number of events in the same line, coming one after another in spatial succession. This means that something that takes place at this point will end precisely at another point. We might go through a series of experiences that seem to have no meaning, connection, or importance. But as we go through the whole process, we come to understand the divine plan that took us from one point of purpose to our next point in time. And it was always in operation.

Sequence is a continuous and connected series. In order for you to sequence something, you must have a sequencer. For example, to sequence music, you must have a sequencer. What is a sequencer? A *sequencer* is "a tool for arranging the events in the life of a single subject." Sequencing makes order out of what appears to be disorder. So then, we can say that God is the sequencer of our lives. How can we say that? *A man's steps are directed by the* LORD (Proverbs 20:24). This means your steps are fixed, fitted, and fashioned by God to accomplish your destiny. What seems to be disorder in your life will eventually be manifested as God's order in your life.

That's why Paul wrote in Romans 8:28 that all things work together for the good of those that love God and have been called according to His purpose. If you look at life in the context of the immediate moment, you might think it has no meaning. But when you look at it in the context of extended time, then it takes on meaning.

God is the sequencer behind the story of Nehemiah. He is the One who is at work behind the scenes. We must always understand that He is the Originator, the Source, and the Foundation of all that we do. If we take any false steps, we get out of sequence, and confusion and disorder follows.

The last word is *succession*. Succession is the right of a person in line to succeed another. It is the act or process of one person taking the place of another person in the enjoyment of their rights. We are talking about inheritance. Power and wisdom extended through the generations has a powerful effect upon the world. A person's influence should extend from one generation to the next. It is like a pebble thrown into a pond that ripples the water and eventually reaches the distant shore.

When you're in the line of succession, you're always positioned *behind* the person God ordained you to *follow after*. When Jesus told His disciples to follow Him, He was saying that if they got in line and followed Him, what He had would become theirs. God acts as the sequencer, creating a series of events that culminate and intensify His purposes through the divine order of succession. God operates in lines.

God operates in the Spirit and in the law of succession. Process leads to promise, provision, and purpose. Through the processes of life, God brings us to the place of blessing. As the blessing is passed on to the next generation, then the purposes of God can be accomplished.

We understand that what we are doing is not the main thing or even the final thing. We live in a series of sequences. The strategy and plan of God is the main thing. You and I are not the main thing. Our lives are simply a contribution to the main thing. Our lives take on meaning as they are connected to the ultimate purposes of God.

John the Baptist understood this principle. He understood that he was standing in a line of succession and that the time was coming when he would decrease in order that the one coming after Him might increase. The one was Jesus, the Christ. John fully understood that the stream of his life was flowing toward a definitive time in history, and once it reached that point, his purpose would be completed.

When God called Abraham, He called a man, and out of that man He formed a nation to himself. Watch the succession. The trans-generational blessing was transferred to Isaac, then Jacob, and finally it was transferred to Joseph. Why? So Joseph could take them into the place of prophetic promise and spiritual provision. But Joseph prophesied in Genesis 50:24 that a time would come when God would take the Jews out of the land of Egypt and lead them to the land He had promised to their forefathers—Abraham, Isaac, and Jacob. The chosen one would be Moses. The anointing on Joseph brought them into Egypt so they could escape the world famine and live in security, but the anointing on Moses would take them into the land of promise. Moses never reached that place, but there was one who came *after* Moses—Joshua—who did bring them into the Promised Land. It is important that we are standing in the place where we should be standing in order that the succession of divine purpose is accomplished.

CHOOSING THE TEAM

The type of men Nehemiah chose to stand with him and work beside him speaks volumes to the type of people we should allow into our lives today.

First, Nehemiah chose priests to oversee the construction, and specifically, he chose the high priest Eliashib to manage a certain section of the wall. Eliashib was the grandson of the priest Joshua, who worked with Zerubbabel in the initial stages of the project. The name *Eliashib* is significant in this passage. It means "my God will restore."

Nehemiah chose priests, men who were close to God and could capture His vision, but he also chose one specific man with a heart for restoration—what Nehemiah's mission was all about. No one can ever deny the power of the second man. It is the second man who often oversees the actual work of the leader, representing his vision and actuating his purposes.

The priestly anointing is the anointing of restoration. The object of a priest is to reconcile people to God, and our great High Priest, Jesus, was the ultimate fulfillment of this priestly role. A huge fissure had been created in the world of man. It was a crack in the relationship between God and man. Because of sin, man was separated from God and his personal destiny. When God apprehends us, He then calls each one of us to become ministers of reconciliation in this world. We are like the second man in that we are carrying out the orders of our King and bringing men and women into harmony with the divine will.

Next to the priests, the men of Jericho were assigned a section of the wall to repair. Historically, these men had been opposed to God's ways, to Jerusalem, and to everything God was doing in the earth. Remember that God does not choose as we would choose. He saw something in these men that others did not see, for God looks on the heart while we in this world judge others based upon the surface. God has a way of wiping out the past and giving us a new destiny.

Next to the men from Jericho, Zaccur, son of Imri, labored on the project. The name *Zaccur* means "to be mindful of, to mention, to remember, to reflect on or talk about." Zaccur was the son of Imri, whose name actually means "talkative." When you've truly been rescued and restored by God, you can't forget it and you certainly can't stop talking about it! Zaccur's testimony was a powerful tool that fired passion, enthusiasm, intensity, and zeal in his fellow workers—and your testimony can be as well!

Working *next to* Zaccur and balancing out his enthusiasm was Hassenaah who was a no-nonsense type of person. The name *Hassenaah* means "to the point." In other words, he did not play with his words. He was direct and not deceitful with his speech. The Hassenaahs among us are those who get serious and stay serious about the things of God. They are focused on the mission and refuse to be distracted from what God has called them to do. They do not get involved in frivolous conversations.

What does all of this have to do with you? It only serves to illustrate that you will be exposed to all kinds of people in your life—people with different personalities and different gifts. It does take all kinds of people to accomplish God's purposes. The God of diversity has created a people of diversity. God's creation is not bland, nondescript, ordinary, and robotic. He created humanity with diversity and variety. Through the diversity of humankind, God will accomplish His purpose and manifest His multifaceted and multicolored glory. When we seek to replicate other people, seeking to be like them, we negate the purposes of God for our lives. God puts people *next to* us not for the purpose of making us like them but for strengthening us to fulfill our own calling.

The priests: Who understands the unique mission to which God has called you? Who provides you with spiritual encouragement and challenges you to rise up and fulfill that mission? Who pours the oil of the anointing of restoration over your life?

The men of Jericho: Whose testimony inspires you? Perhaps it is someone you know personally or simply someone you have read about—in the Bible or in your local newspaper. Whose story gives you strength to complete the mission of your own life? And here is a more difficult question: Who are *you* inspiring through *your* testimony?

Zaccur and Imri: Is there someone in your inner circle who fires you up and motivates you to keep on keepin' on? We all need people who will continually remind us of the powerful works of God that have occurred in the past and of the amazing things that are going to happen in the future.

Hassenaah: Who helps you stay focused on what God has called you to do? In a world filled with distractions, we all need someone who can keep us on task and tuned in to the call God has placed on our lives.

Who have you allowed into your inner circle of influence? Who is next to you? Who are you next to? Trust, honor, duty, integrity, and courage; these are the things that make men great. When you discover who will develop and celebrate these traits in you, then and only then will you begin to tap into the "power of next."

CHARACTER SKETCH— INFLUENCE

John Wesley

JOHN WESLEY WAS BORN IN 1703 and died in 1791. Like Martin Luther, Wesley's life and ministry created a dramatic shift in the course of Christianity. Wesley was a powerful preacher and teacher, and he took that power to the streets, fields, and remote places where no other Anglican preacher would go. But Wesley did not go alone. He took laymen with him, organizing and instructing them on how to witness and minister to his generation of the lost.

"Methodism had three rises, the first at Oxford University with the founding of the so-called 'Holy Club,' the second while Wesley was parish priest in Savannah, Georgia, and the third in London after Wesley's return to England."[6] While attending Oxford, Wesley became the leader of a band of young Oxford students who were passionate for the cause of Christ. His younger brother, Charles, who shared a similar passion for Jesus and compassion for the lost, had originally started this band of disciples called the Holy Club. They would later be referred to as "Methodists" because of their method of reading and studying the Bible and their charitable acts. In fact, the theology of Wesley was a practical theology that led him to fight on behalf of those who sat on the outer fringes of society.

John Wesley had been ordained for more than ten years but had not had many successes in his ministry. He had been to America, but had failed miserably as a missionary to Georgia. He returned to England with a heavy heart, saddened by his lack of power and influence. He went to a church meeting and someone began to read from Luther's preface to the book of Romans. The preface describes what happens when one opens his heart in simple faith to the living God. This simple revelation hit Wesley like a lightening bolt and changed his life and ministry forever. Later, Wesley described his life-changing experience when he wrote these classic words: "I felt my heart strangely warmed. I felt I did trust in Christ, Christ alone, for salvation, and an assurance was given me that he had taken away my sins, even mine, and saved me from the law of sin and death."[7] Strangely warm—the warmth that was generated in his heart that night was about to set all England ablaze with glorious revival.

At the age of thirty-five, his life was changed, and there would be no going back to the old ways of religion. The direction for his life would now be set on a new path—one that would focus on this message of faith in Christ. He would know for the rest of his life that the God who is reflected in the face of Jesus Christ had come down to earth to visit him and had done for Wesley precisely what he could never have done for himself. His earlier zeal for holy living would remain with him, but it would be enhanced with an intense thankfulness for the grace and mercy given to him—a grace and mercy that was not based upon any work that he had ever done, but on Christ's work alone.

The results among the people who heard the "new" Wesley were immediate. Wesley preached with a new power, and the people were pulled into the Kingdom by his dynamic presentation of the gospel of Christ. Hundreds and then thousands who were vacillating between pompous pride and deadly despair now accepted Christ and immediately experienced an assurance of their new lives as children of God.

Wesley had his enemies, but they were not among those in the fields. They lived in the ecclesiastical realms of dead religion. They wasted no time harassing him. Pulpits were closed to him. Wesley had no choice. His parish would now become the world. He had always considered the fields to be a despicable place for any preacher. But now, influenced by his friend George Whitefield, he would launch his preaching outside the church walls, and people responding to Wesley's preaching would quickly fill those fields. Wesley was soon preaching the gospel to thousands of people who would never have entered the doors of any church. The path of disillusionment had now turned into a highway of influence.

"Wesley…attended to the sick, the dying, the imprisoned, and the forgotten…. Faced with the ravages of eighteenth-century poverty…he spent himself tirelessly on behalf of the socially submerged. In 1746 he established the first free pharmacy in London. Haunted especially by the plight of widows, he reconditioned two small homes for them. Outraged that his people were denied access to banks, he scraped together fifty pounds and began assisting those who needed small amounts of investment capital.

"It is impossible to exaggerate the hardships Wesley sustained: 250,000 miles on horseback, 40,000 sermons preached without amplification, 22 crossings of the Irish Sea, exposure to inclement weather, hostility from those with vested interests, life-long conflict from those who disdained his vehement rejection of predestination and his equally vehement insistence on godliness."[8]

Wesley—as Nehemiah of old—realized that he would not be able to accomplish the task by himself. He would need others to stand *next to* him. "Wesley's followers first met in private home 'societies.' When these societies became too large for members to care for one another, Wesley organized 'classes,' each with 11 members and a leader. Classes met weekly to pray, read the Bible, discuss their spiritual lives, and to collect money for charity. Men and women met separately, but anyone could become a class leader."[9]

These classes and societies would not have been held together without Wesley's system of traveling lay preachers. "The itinerants were taught to manage difficulties in the societies, to face mobs, to brave any weather, to subsist without means, except as might casually occur on their routes, to rise at four and preach at five o'clock, to scatter books and tracts, to live by rule, and to die without fear."[10]

Records reflect the exact number of followers Wesley had at the time of his death: "294 preachers, 71,668 British members, 19 missionaries (5 in mission stations), and 43,265 American members with 198 preachers. Today Methodists numbers about 30 million worldwide."[11]

The influence of Wesley and his band of preachers would change the face of England forever, lifting it out of the ruts of religion and ditches of despair. He faced the enemies of the cross with great honor and fueled the fires of revival throughout England. Eventually those fires would spread to American shores, and his name would forever be locked in the annals of church history as the man who influenced a whole nation. But he could not have done it alone. With the support of his mighty band of disciples Wesley was able to influence the whole world and we continue to feel that impact to this very day.

Greater love has no one than this, that
he lay down his life for his friends.
You are my friends if you do what
I command. I no longer call you
servants, because a servant does not
know his master's business. Instead, I
have called you friends, for everything
that I learned from my Father I have
made known to you. You did not choose
me, but I chose you and appointed you
to go and bear fruit—fruit that will last.

Jesus, the Gospel of John

CHAPTER TWO

THE POWER OF AGREEMENT— COVENANT

 HERE IS A WORD NESTLED sweetly in the prophetic words of Amos 3:3, KJV. *Can two walk together, except they be agreed?* The word *agree* is one of the most underestimated and overlooked words in all of Scripture. To Jesus it was imperial to His mission, to the prophet it was intended for his prophetic focus, and to the church today it is imperative for our future. With it, we can build and grow; without it, we struggle and are frustrated. With it, we are united; without it, we are divided.

Nehemiah knew the power of agreement when he set out to rebuild the wall at Jerusalem. He did not embark on the God-ordained adventure with the words, "I will." Rather, he chose to intrinsically motivate God's people with the words, "Let us." Churches today would enjoy much more success and experience less frustration if they would only focus their concentrated efforts on agreement.

Christianity is about confluence—the flowing of our lives together and all streams coming together to build one powerful river. All human activity is under the gravitational pull of heaven pulling our individual efforts into one dynamic center that will promote the cause of Christ and move the world toward His ultimate goal.

Purpose cannot be accomplished if there is no agreement—a concurrence of many wills that submits to the divine will. Agreement is the foundation upon which purpose can be worked out. In the basement of agreement, purpose can be established, and then plans are developed that become the superstructure for changing the world. It all starts with an agreement—a covenant.

AGREEMENT—THE HEAVENLY WAY

The way of agreement is the heavenly way. *For there are three that testify: the Spirit, the water and the blood; and the three are in agreement* (1 John 5:7-8). Heaven is arranged in total agreement concerning the purpose of Christ. In earth three agree: the Spirit, the blood and water. Together they sing in three-part harmony with the three-fold testimony of heaven. What are they agreeing on? They agree on the divine plan that is the manifestation of the ultimate purpose. The purpose is to bring all things back into original unity. The plan is Christ. They are agreeing—bearing witness to the fact that no one can come to the Father except through the Son.

This "bearing witness" had been described before in the gospel of John. Jesus, in one of His many face-offs with the Pharisees, was challenged to prove his credibility as the Son of God: *When Jesus spoke again to the people, He said, "I am the light of the world. Whoever follows me will never walk in dark-*

ness, but will have the light of life." The Pharisees challenged him, "Here you are, appearing as your own witness; your testimony is not valid." Jesus answered, "Even if I testify on my own behalf, my testimony is valid, for I know where I came from and where I am going. But you have no idea where I come from or where I am going. You judge by human standards; I pass judgment on no one. But if I do judge, my decisions are right, because I am not alone. I stand with the Father, who sent me. In your own Law it is written that the testimony of two men is valid. I am one who testifies for myself; my other witness is the Father, who sent me" (John 8:12-18).

The Pharisees told Jesus that no one except Jesus could attest to the fact that He was sent of the Father. Jesus' response simply stated that He and God know who He is and where He came from and that is enough to confirm the truth. He then cited a principle of the Pharisees that says if two people say something is true then it's true.

Once again, the Son demonstrates His confidence in the power of agreement by showing that He and His Father are one. By the power of agreement, truth is established and when truth is established, covenant can be formed. There can be no covenant or bonding or relationships without truth. Truth is the fabric of relationships that can be fashioned into covenants. At the headwaters of truth there is the Father, the Son, and the Spirit who have confirmed and testified to all truth. What they have testified to then becomes the stream that flows into the rivers of covenant.

COVENANT—THE POWER OF AGREEMENT

Covenant works essentially in two dimensions, two dynamics. First, it involves the relationship between God and human beings. The covenant between God and man establishes the basis of that relationship. This covenant is not like human covenants that are negotiated. This covenant is not negotiated between two equal parties, but it is initiated and established by God's loving determination. He is the initiator and man is the responder. Secondly, covenant involves relationship between humans. It is the basis of all human friendships. It sets the criteria by which human relationships function—agreement, loyalty, friendship, honesty, commitment, and all human functions.

Covenant is not only a relational word, but it is also a redemptive word. When man broke his agreement with God, it created a fissure in all relationships. First, man's relationship with God was broken. Man became estranged from God. This break in the vertical relationship would have tragic effects upon the human relationship, and before long man was killing man.

In order to repair the relationship side of covenant, there must be redemption. The covenant of redemption restores the covenant of relationships. In order for relationships to be repaired, there must be a repairing of the relationship between God and man, for God is the source of all that makes human relationships what they should be. The Gospel is the good news that all relationships can be healed.

NO PREJUDICE, NO SEPARATION

The divine covenant between God and man is the foundation for all human covenants. Once there is union between God and man, there can and must be union in the human arena. The divine covenant insists that all human relationships be healed. Segregation and prejudice stand as enemies to the cause of Christ because they violate the covenant of redemption. Within the human drama, man has isolated himself within the collective clique.

Under the covering of our prized groups we find a comfort and acceptance for our prejudice against those outside our paradigms. Jesus came to destroy the collective clique and tear down all walls that divide men. All prejudice and separation of men into groupings is a violation of the principle of the Body and the purpose of redemption. In Galatians 3:28, Paul declares, *There is neither Jew nor Greek, slave nor free, male nor female, for you are all one in Christ Jesus.*

There is a certain divine power and joy that is released within the community of God when discrimination is defeated and segregation is silenced. Man can never come into the power of agreement as long as he is plagued with prejudice and any form of bigotry that creates division within the human family. Our minds must be renewed and our hearts softened so that we are able to embrace all in the family of man. Once our pride is eliminated, we will find the place where we can become one with others. How could this happen? It will take the fire of adversity to make that agreement complete and break jealousy and prejudice.

COVENANT FOUND IN THE FIRE

A friend loves at all times, and a brother is born for adversity (Proverbs 17:17). A friend means "an associate or companion; someone who is close to you." Friends are associated with you. But what makes them a true friend is their love. When do they love? At all times. A good friend has deep affection for you. It is not a passive relationship. It is a relationship that has depth based on love.

As we move to the second part of the verse, we observe a certain ascension in thought, moving from friend to brother. There is a deepening in commitment and a transformation of the relationship. The catalyst is adversity. The result of the adversity is—a brother. In the fires of adversity covenant is born and a brother is found. In times of prosperity, our friends will know us, but in times of adversity we will know our friends.

It is when you face an adversary, staring into the face of opposition with anguish gripping your heart, that you need a friend to become your brother. He was born for that very moment, in order to stand with you and encourage you and lift you up. While others are fleeing the burning house, he is racing in to save you from your trouble. A brother will refresh you while you're in prison. Second Timothy 1:16 encourages us to be faithful. It says, *May the Lord show mercy to the household of Onesiphorus, because he often refreshed me and was not ashamed of my chains.*

In other words, Timothy was saying, "Be a blessing to this friend of mine, Onesiphorus. Why? He wasn't ashamed of me while I was in prison, and more than that he stood with me and refreshed my spirit and lifted me up." Friendships advance to new levels of strength and importance during times of adversity.

The greatest example of brotherhood born in adversity is found in the relationship between Jonathan and David. These two young men had a very special friendship that was sealed with a covenant. They loved each other and their souls were bound to one another. King Saul would test this relationship mightily and repeatedly. Saul's jealousy drove David out of the house and into the woods. But anyone can handle the woods as long as they know they've got a brother in the house. For years this friendship would survive the fire of Saul's intense jealousy.

Jonathan was always there for David, and the intensity of that relationship is manifested at the death of Jonathan.

DEATH OF A FRIEND

In 2 Samuel 1:17-21, after hearing of the death of Saul and Jonathan on the battlefield, we read, *David took up this lament concerning Saul and his son Jonathan, and ordered that the men of Judah be taught this lament of the bow (it is written in the Book of Jashar): "Your glory, O Israel, lies slain on your heights. How the mighty have fallen! Tell it not in Gath, proclaim it not in the streets of Ashkelon, lest the daughters of the Philistines be glad, lest the daughters of the uncircumcised rejoice. O mountains of Gilboa, may you have neither dew nor rain, nor fields that yield offerings [of grain]. For there the shield of the mighty was defiled, the shield of Saul—no longer rubbed with oil."*

When David wrote this, every word was stained with his tears. Verses 22 through 27 continue, *From the blood of the slain, from the flesh of the mighty, the bow of Jonathan did not turn back, the sword of Saul did not return unsatisfied. Saul and Jonathan—in life they were loved and gracious, and in death they were not parted. They were swifter than eagles, they were stronger than lions. O daughters of Israel, weep for Saul, who clothed you in scarlet and finery, who adorned your garments with ornaments of gold. How the mighty have fallen in battle! Jonathan lies slain on your heights. I grieve for you, Jonathan my brother; you were very dear to me. Your love for me was wonderful, more wonderful than that of women. How the mighty have fallen! The weapons of war have perished!*

David was deeply distressed by the loss of his brother. He hurt for Jonathan. In the fire of affliction their souls had been forged together, and they grew up believing that nothing could ever separate them. Now David felt the pain of this tragic separation. Jonathan had been more than a friend—he had become a *brother* to David. Over and over again Jonathan had protected David from Saul. Jonathan covered David's back, risking the love of his own father.

A brother is more than just a friend. A brother is someone who will stay at your side even in the face of adversity. Brothers are not necessarily connected in commonality, but they will connect in the face of confrontation. Every one of us needs a friend, a brother who has been born in the midst of adversity and can stand with us in the fire of tribulation.

Besides needing such a friend, we must *become* somebody's brother. We are born to become a brother for someone else. Not only do we need a friend, but we must also learn to become a friend. While learning to become a friend, we might just find that friend we seek. When one brother is joined to another, they become a band of brothers, and the power of the band cannot be broken.

The army of England's King Henry V at Agincourt had been reduced to a small band of tired and weary men. Many of them were wounded. Outnumbered five to one, Henry rallied his troops to his side by reminding them that they were not mercenaries, but a "band of brothers."

> *We few, we happy few, we band of brothers;*
> *For he to-day that sheds his blood with me*
> *Shall be my brother...*
> *And gentlemen in England, now a-bed*
> *Shall think themselves accursed they were not here;*
> *And hold their manhoods cheap whiles any speaks*
> *That fought with us....*
> —Shakespeare, *Henry V*

Yes, we need men to whom we can bare our souls. But it isn't going to happen with a group of guys you don't trust and who really aren't willing to go to battle with you. It's a long-standing truth that there is never a more devoted group of men than those who have fought alongside one another, the men of your squadron, the guys in your foxhole. It will never be a large group, but we don't need a large group.

A COVENANT BENEFITS FUTURE GENERATIONS

The covenant forged between David and Jonathan didn't just apply to them—it applied to the future generations of their families. It is extremely important to find out the one that God has assigned to be *next to* you in your life, because when you align your life with theirs, God will protect even your children in crippled conditions.

The covenant forged by David and Jonathan would extend into the next generation:

> *Then Jonathan said to David… "May the LORD be with you as he has been with my father. But show me unfailing kindness like that of the LORD as long as I live, so that I may not be killed, and do not ever cut off your kindness from my family—not even when the LORD has cut off every one of David's enemies from the face of the earth." So Jonathan made a covenant with the house of David, saying, "May the LORD call David's enemies to account." And Jonathan had David reaffirm his oath out of love for him, because he loved him as he loved himself.*
>
> —1 Samuel 20:12-17

Years later, even after his friend Jonathan had been killed in battle, David longed to honor his covenant with his fallen brother and asked his servants to find any of Jonathan's relatives whom he could bless.

> *Now there was a servant of Saul's household named Ziba. They called him to appear before David, and the king said to him, "Are you Ziba?"*
>
> *"Your servant," he replied.*
>
> *The king asked, "Is there no one still left of the house of Saul to whom I can show God's kindness?"*
>
> *Ziba answered the king, "There is still a son of Jonathan; he is crippled in both feet."*
>
> *"Where is he?" the king asked.*
>
> *Ziba answered, "He is at the house of Makir son of Ammiel in Lo Debar."*
>
> —2 Samuel 9:2-4

Jonathan's son, Mephibosheth, was living in an obscure, barren part of Palestine, hidden away because of his affiliation with King Saul and the crippling condition he had suffered since childhood described in 2 Samuel 4:4: *Jonathan son of Saul had a son who was lame in both feet. He was five years old when the news about Saul and Jonathan came from Jezreel. His nurse picked him up and fled, but as she hurried to leave, he fell and became crippled. His name was Mephibosheth.*

When this frightened man was brought into David's presence, he threw down his crutches and fell, trembling before the king. But David said: *"Don't be afraid…for I will surely show you kindness for the sake of your father Jonathan. I will restore to you all the land that belonged to your grandfather Saul, and you will always eat at my table"* (2 Samuel 9:7).

Rather than feeling the sword upon his neck as he had expected, Mephibosheth experienced the power of covenant, *the power of next*, as David reached out his hand from above and lifted Mephibosheth to his feet.

A COVENANT OF BROTHERS

In 2 Samuel 5:10-12, we find another powerful story of covenant that succeeded into the next generation. *And he [David] became more and more powerful, because the Lord God Almighty was with him. Now Hiram king of Tyre sent messengers to David, along with cedar logs and carpenters and stonemasons, and they built a palace for David. And David knew that the Lord had established him as king over Israel and had exalted his kingdom for the sake of his people Israel.*

God provided a man for David's life to connect with him in covenant in order that he could fulfill his destiny. David could not do it alone, and Hiram came on the scene as a brother of covenant who would provide what David lacked in fulfilling his purpose in life.

God has a covenant that He is establishing in each of our lives. We cannot fulfill our destiny on our own. We will need some provisions that are not in our hand—provisions to which we have no access. Here's the good news. God will provide a "Hiram" for you, someone who will enable you to fulfill God's plan for your life.

The covenant of the brotherhood was so strong between Hiram and David that when David died, Hiram switched his allegiance to David's son, Solomon. The compassion they had for each other had extended into the next generation. Hiram forever loved David and was loyal to His cause. He loved Solomon because he had loved David. So Hiram let Solomon know that he would help him complete the work of his father.

Solomon responded, *"You know that because of the wars waged against my father David from all sides, he could not build a temple for the Name of the Lord his God until the Lord put his enemies under his feet. But now the Lord my God has given me rest on every side, and there is no adversary or disaster. I intend, therefore, to build a temple for the Name of the Lord my God, as the Lord told my father David, when he said, 'Your son whom I will put on the throne in your place will build the temple for my Name'"* (1 Kings 5:3-5).

What he just said was that his father had won all the battles. He had won those battles for his son, for this day, so that Solomon could complete the work that God had given him to do. He cleared the way for David's son. Then it dawned on Solomon that the relationship David had with Hiram was for this day. The power of their friendship would enable Solomon to complete the task.

Without any sense of embarrassment, he could freely ask Hiram to provide the cedars of Lebanon for the building of the house of God. When Hiram heard Solomon's words he was overwhelmed with joy. Hiram recognized that the favor upon David was now resting upon his son Solomon and agreed to provide what Solomon needed. Solomon then responded to Hiram's gracious act and reciprocated by year after year giving him wheat and oil and thus a covenant was formed, a bond was created.

A covenant of brotherhood is a relationship with another that cannot be broken, an affinity toward each other that is compassionate and kind, and a commitment to the future success of one another. It is all persons engaged in a particular purpose or cause, both male and female. This constitutes the brotherhood—the covenant that cannot be broken but must always be guarded.

DANGER ZONE—FAVOR CAUSES JEALOUSY

Within the bonds of covenant there is one human passion that can break the band—jealousy. As you travel through Scripture you become aware of the evil energy of jealousy lurking around every corner. This injurious influence affected the first human family. When Cain saw the favor that was on his brother, Abel, he did not react out of compassion but out of covetousness. Rather than being drawn in love to his brother's favor, he was repelled by the force of favor that his brother enjoyed. Cain took the ultimate action of a jealous man by killing his brother in the field. Beware of what favor on your life might do to the one *next* to you.

In Genesis 37 we read about the tragic events that led to Joseph's brothers selling him into slavery. Jacob sent Joseph into the fields (bad things can happen in the field) to find his brothers. Directed by a stranger, Joseph headed for Dothan. He thought he was going to find his brothers and see how they were doing. He hoped they might be able to help him follow his dream.

Instead of finding help from his brothers, he found hatred and jealousy and fell into their plot to kill him. The plot was adjusted to selling him into slavery. The brothers could not bear the favor that was on Joseph's life. It was a burden rather than a blessing—a burden that they must get rid of. Unfortunately, favor shown to one can manifest evil in another. Not all are able to walk in the covenant of brotherhood. It seems that there will always be that one who will be offended by the favor and will seek to take your life rather than serve your life. The good news is that there will be those who are born as brothers in adversity and will be with you forever. Be wise in the decisions that you make concerning those who enter your life.

You and I desperately need a band of brothers who are willing to shed their blood with us—to stand with us and lift us up when we need them, and those whom we can lift up when they have fallen. It is true that one can put a thousand to flight, but two can put ten thousand to flight. This is the power of agreement—an agreement forged in the fire of adversity resulting in a covenant that will extend to the next generations.

CHARACTER SKETCH—COVENANT

William Wallace

Sir William Wallace of Elerslie, hero of Scotland and true patriot, his desire for peace and freedom united the clans, gained the loyalty of the people, struck fear into his enemies and defied the cruel hand of an evil, warring and invading King— Edward "Longshanks" Plantagenet I of England.

—Author Unknown

WILLIAM WALLACE EMERGED OUT OF the shadows of myth into the bright lights of reality through the success of Mel Gibson's 1995 film, *Braveheart*. For the Scottish people who hold him in great honor, he is revered as a freedom fighter, passionate patriot, and an icon of Scottish independence. Through his valiant efforts concluding with the sacrifice of his own life, Wallace was able to forge together the many tribes of Scotland into one mighty force. His life was a rallying point for all Scots to join together in covenant, and stand against those who would invade their land, and control their rights to live as free men.

"Wallace was born around 1270, probably near Ellerslie (now Elderslie), in Ayrshire, Scotland. His father was Sir Malcolm Wallace, Laird of Elderslie and Auchinbothie, a small landowner and little-known Scottish knight…His mother is believed to have been the daughter of Sir Hugh Crawford, Sheriff of Ayr, and he is thought to have had an elder brother, also called Malcolm. Because he was the second son, William did not inherit his father's title or lands."[1]

Unlike the other potential leaders of the Scots in the fourteenth century, Wallace was of ordinary birth. He was a mere warrior and could not be compared to the aristocratic importance of someone like Robert the Bruce. But Wallace would emerge out of the masses of mere mortals and become a great leader who would liberate Scotland from the imposed bondage of British rule. His very existence was a continual threat to the invaders, due to his uncompromising views and actions tied by a covenant of the heart to Scotland, the land of his birth.

When Wallace was in his late teens, entering his early twenties, Scotland was ruled by the English, and they experienced internal conflict as the Scottish aristocracy fought amongst each other, each desiring to rule over Scotland. There was no national unity, no peace, and no leader to help them gain their freedom. Their British occupiers were ruthless and brutal, and there was no rule of law and no protection of the rights of the common Scot.

"While a teenaged William received his education in the church, his father and older brother were on the run from the English. Sir Malcolm refused to swear allegiance to King

Edward (Longshanks) as Scottish landowners were required to do. Civil conflict continued to heat up in Scotland, and in 1291, Sir Malcolm was killed [in] a battle at Loudoun Hill."[2]

Wallace's hatred of the English, no doubt, started with the death of his father, and at this point in time it appears that he awoke to his coming destiny. His destiny became complete when an English sheriff killed his longtime sweetheart. Wallace began to gather young and old Scots to his side. They were mesmerized by the power of his passion for the Scottish cause. In Wallace they discovered a man that they could follow. His rally was not to a piece of paper, but a covenant of the heart and of kinsman. He was much different than the ruling Scottish aristocrats who seemed to only care about establishing their own positions of power. Wallace had only one passion—a liberated and free Scotland!

"Gathering men around him as his rebellion gathered momentum, Wallace's greatest victory came at the Battle of Stirling Bridge. This 1297 rout of the larger English force brought Wallace to national prominence."[3]

Throughout the years leading up to the time of Wallace, the Scottish nobility had felt that they must give in to English demands for allegiance. Wallace's actions were exposing their weakness and cowardice. Wallace's patriotic force of commoners remained unequivocally dedicated to the struggle for Scottish independence and would not bend to the wishes of the aristocrats who wanted to compromise with England in order to preserve their place and power.

As Wallace grew in his power, the nobility of Scotland sought to create a compromise with Edward. Since Robert the Bruce could not secure an alliance with the French, he was forced to compromise with King Edward in 1302. Wallace would not submit to any compromise. He was committed to live in a Scotland that was free from British rule. It was quite clear that Wallace had made a covenant with Scotland, and because of that covenant he would not bow to the British king, even if it meant losing his life.

Once Edward had won the support of Robert the Bruce, he immediately sought to capture Wallace, pronouncing him an outlaw and traitor. "A ransom of 300 Merks was offered for the capture of Wallace, and Edward's captains and governors were issued with strict orders to use every endeavor to capture him and send him in chains to London. By the treachery of one of his servants named Jack Short, Wallace was betrayed, according to legend, into the hands of a Scottish Baron, John Monteith."[4]

Wallace was taken to London, and there he was executed as a traitor. Dragged to the execution place, he was hung, drawn, and quartered. His head was mounted on a traitor's gate, and the pieces of his body were sent to Newcastle, Berwick, Perth, and Stirling.[5]

Wallace's refusal to settle for anything less than complete independence for his beloved Scotland became a rallying point for the beleaguered Scots. Inspired by his death, they would rise up until they eventually saw the birth of freedom. Forever, Wallace will be remembered as one who united his brothers under a cry for freedom. He forged a band of brothers who fought for the freedom of Scotland.

Wallace's unwavering commitment to freedom and Scotland influenced others to value commitment, truth, and covenant.

I am William Wallace, and I see a whole army
of my countrymen here, in defiance of tyranny.
You've come to fight as free men, and free men you

are. What will you do with that freedom? Will you fight? Fight and you may die, run and you'll live. At least a while. And dying in your beds, many years from now, would you be willing to trade all the days, from this day to that, for one chance, just one chance, to come back here and tell our enemies that they may take away our lives, but they'll never take our freedom![6]

Two are better than one, because they
have a good return for their work:
If one falls down, his friend can help
him up. But pity the man who falls
and has no one to help him up!

–King Solomon, Ecclesiastes 4:9, 10

CHAPTER THREE

O Brother, Where Art Thou?— Friendship

 S WE HAVE ALREADY SEEN in the life of Joseph, it is possible for us to reject the very brother who is the key to our future. The favor that we are jealous of will become the very favor that will save our lives. When we cry out, "Brother, where art thou?" we will sadly discover that we sold our deliverer, our brother, our friend into slavery. The awesome thing about God is that He is a Redeemer. He takes what we have destroyed by our jealous actions and redeems it—buys it back—and by the power of His love and wisdom, transforms it into our deliverance. That is the power of a Friend who brings forth new friends into our lives.

David, the shepherd, did not leave his father's household to set out on a journey to find Goliath. He went looking for his brothers, and on the way he found Goliath and his destiny. When God has a mission and a mandate and has dropped a mantle on someone's life, there will always be a confrontation on the journey to fulfill his destiny. David walked through some conflict before he found a true brother. Sometimes those of our own family will not be the brothers that we will need on the journey to fulfilling our purpose. Jesus' own brothers rejected Him and did not understand who He was and what He was destined to become. But a little band of misfits would become His brothers, and it would be these seemingly insignificant followers who would help Him change the course of the world.

TROUBLE—THE PATHWAY TO A FRIEND
David and Jonathan

When you discover your purpose, get ready to face some problems. Purpose will lead you to problems, and the problems will lead you to a provision of grace dressed up as a friend. But your problems should not discourage you. Your problems should encourage you, knowing that as you pass through the pathway of pain it will lead you into the place of purpose.

Problems, difficulties, struggles, pain, and obstacles in life will confound our careful theories and theological certainties. They confront our calculations and contradict our generalizations. Just when we think we've found the formula to fit the facts, something unpredictable and unconventional appears in our lives, making our logic look absurd and irrelevant. We think we have established the rule only to discover a host of exceptions.

David goes to find his brothers, and on the way he finds a giant—a giant who is standing in his way to finding a friend who would serve his destiny. In slaying the giant, God opened the door for David into the palace, providing the opportunity for him to discover Jonathan, who would become his friend and brother. Everyone needs a friend, someone that will walk through hell with him. But sometimes we have to walk through hell to find that brother. *O brother, where art thou?* The friend you need is often found in the fire of adversity.

Paul and Titus

> *Now when I went to Troas to preach the gospel of Christ and found that the Lord had opened a door for me, I still had no peace of mind, because* **I did not find my brother Titus there.** *So I said good-by to them and went on to Macedonia. For when we came into Macedonia, this body of ours had no rest, but we were harassed at every turn—conflicts on the outside, fears within. But God, who comforts the downcast, comforted us by the coming of Titus, and not only by his coming but also by the comfort you had given him.*
> —2 Corinthians 2:12,13; 7:5-7, emphasis added

Every one of us needs agents of encouragement who God strategically fits into the puzzle of our destiny, helping us to be resurrected from the grace of grief and get us back on the pathway to our promise.

After trying to push into Phrygia and Bithynia, Paul arrived at Troas. He could not get a sense of what would be the next direction for his life. While sleeping, he saw a man from Macedonia pleading with him to come over and help him. Paul awakened the next morning with a new sense of purpose and destiny. The way was clear. He would go to Macedonia.

Opposition confronted him when he arrived at Philippi. After the conversion of Lydia's household and the deliverance of a young girl possessed by demons, the town reacted and came after Paul and Silas. They ripped their clothes off, beat them, and threw them into prison. By a miraculous intervention, they got out of prison and headed for Thessalonica. And after some success they were run out of town again. Paul arrived in the city of Corinth and had his greatest success there and remained in Corinth for eighteen months before leaving for Ephesus. He was able to establish a vibrant church in Ephesus but again he faced opposition. Everywhere Paul went, opposition followed.

Finally, toward the end of his apostolic travels, he arrived at Troas a second time. He was worn down from all of his travels, the persecution he had endured, and the concern he had for the churches—especially the church at Corinth. Tired and weary, he wrote these words, *...our flesh had no rest, but there was trouble on every side; without were fightings, within were fears. Nevertheless, God...comforted us...* (2 Corinthians 7:5,6 KJV). There are certain contradictions in life. Unbelievable pressure is pushing into the very soul of this great apostle.

He could feel the force of fear pressing in on his spirit, and outwardly he was being beaten down by persecution. Yet in the midst of that, Paul had learned the paradox of walking with God. In this second letter to the Corinthians, he wrote these memorable words, *Sorrowful, yet always rejoicing; poor, yet making many rich; having nothing, and yet possessing everything* (2 Corinthians 6:10).

Life is a paradox. The yoke is easy and the burden is light, and yet there are times when we feel that we can no longer endure the burdens of living in this world. We bear one another's burden, yet we must bear our own burden. We are citizens of this world, members of the earthly society with ties and responsibilities, yet our citizenship is in heaven. We pursue God, but the real truth is that He is pursuing us.

When I want to do what is good, evil is right there with me. One side of me wants God more than anything, but then there's this other side. So this paradox is inescapable. Like each of us, Paul was fighting on the outside and full of fear on the inside.

What is the source of this fear? He has just written the most difficult letter in his life—a letter to the Corinthians, rebuking them for the immorality and discord that was destroying their testimony. He's fighting to stand for the truth. He's warring for right. In the midst of this spiritual war that is all around him, Paul testifies in 2 Corinthians 4:8, *We are hard pressed on every side, but not crushed; perplexed, but not in despair...* How will Paul fight this fight, and how will he win this spiritual war that has engaged him?

In 2 Corinthians 10:2-4, he says, *I beg you that when I come I may not have to be as bold as I expect to be toward some people who think that we live by the standards of this world. For though we live in the world, we do not wage war as the world does. The weapons we fight with are not the weapons of the world. On the contrary, they have divine power to demolish strongholds.*

Even though we walk in the flesh, we don't war in the flesh. That's a paradox of life. We walk in the flesh, but we do not war in the flesh. The things that are giving us trouble right now are not people and circumstances. They are principalities, powers, rulers and authorities in heavenly realms. If we would stop talking to the person and start talking to the power behind him, then we would start noticing a change in the person!

On the inside, Paul is full of fear. He's not sure of the success of this letter to the Corinthians. He's fearful because he has no idea how they have responded to his message. Will they reject him? Fear is a horrible thing. Fear and faith are both attractive. What you *fear* the most is coming at you. What you *faith* the most is coming at you.

"What I feared has come upon me," Job said in chapter 3 verse 25 of the Old Testament book that bears his name. Now, we also understand that what you *faith* the most is coming at you. *There is no fear in love. But perfect love drives out fear, because fear has to do with punishment. The one who fears is not made perfect in love* (1 John 4:18). The force of love interrupts the encroachment of fear upon our souls.

In the midst of his fear and pain, Paul broke down and boldly declared, *Praise be to the God and Father of our Lord Jesus Christ, the Father of compassion and the God of all comfort, who comforts us in all our troubles, so that we can comfort those in any trouble with the comfort we ourselves have received from God. For just as the sufferings of Christ flow over into our lives, so also through Christ our comfort overflows. If we are distressed, it is for your comfort and salvation; if we are comforted, it is for your comfort, which produces in you patient endurance of the same sufferings we suffer. And our hope for you is firm, because we know that just as you share in our sufferings, so also you share in our comfort* (2 Corinthians 1:3-7).

He uses that word *comfort* five times. The Greek word is *paraclete*, which means "the alongside one." The Holy Spirit is the ultimate "alongside one," but there are others in our lives who become "the alongside ones." There is also a comforting that comes to us when we are going through trouble on every side. It comes through the vehicle of a friend, a brother. No man should be an island. He must find the one who will encourage him and extend a hand to him in his time of trouble.

Paul had no rest, no peace. He could not find Titus. His soul was agitated and longed for his friend. Where was he? Paul went to Macedonia where he finally found Titus. What a glorious day! Paul was encouraged and deeply moved by this reunion. This was exactly what he needed to calm the troubled waters inside him.

There is a profound difference between *associations* and *assignments*. We all have associates in life, people whose paths we casually cross. But an assignment is someone who is destined to be attached to you for a purpose. It is someone in your life who is there to tell you that the hand of God is all over you…that you're blessed in the city and blessed in the field, and you're blessed when you come and blessed when you go. You are the head and not the tail, and you are fearfully and wonderfully made. There's nobody like you in the whole wide world. These kinds of friends are those who know how to weep with us when sorrow has embraced our lives—they know how to speak the right words to bring light into our darkness and to guide us out of the valley of trouble. **Your company is always helping you or hindering you.**

Noah and his sons

In Genesis 9, we find a very interesting story from the life of Noah. He has built a wonderful garden full of grapes. The time came when the grapes had fermented and were ready to be made into wine. He served himself some wine, went into his tent, and got so drunk that he got naked. His son, Ham, saw his father's nakedness and went and told his brothers who were on the outside. Noah had enough trust in Ham to let him be on the inside.

Now, here is an important point to remember. It's always those who you willingly expose yourself to who present the greatest potential to hurt you. Ham should have covered his father's nakedness, protecting him from exposure to those on the outside.

The brothers who were on the outside came in backward with a garment and covered their father's nakedness. Suddenly positions changed. The two who were on the outside were now inside, and the one who was on the inside is now on the outside.

The two outsiders covered their father with a garment they had taken into the tent. The Hebrew word for garment, *simlah*, means "mantle." Their father, who had taken off his mantle, was re-mantled by his two sons. Here is the application. Unfortunately, the people who should be covering your nakedness—protecting you from the ones on the outside—are the ones who end up exposing you to those on the outside.

This is a principle of the body of Christ that should not be broken. *What you know about somebody else does not give you the liberty to tell anybody else.* Your companions can impact your life. Is it important what kind of people you hang out with and allow into the living room of your heart? Those around you might expose you or cover you. We need friends who will cover us in our nakedness.

Peter and John

On their release, Peter and John went back to their own people and reported all that the chief priests and elders had said to them (Acts 4:23). Peter and John were under serious threat. Why? They were being threatened because they were preaching Jesus. As soon as they were let go, they headed straight for the company of their friends. Company, *idios*, means "one's own private people; a group of companions."

A companion is someone who matches another. In John 14:16,17 Jesus said, "*I will ask the Father, and he will give you another Counselor to be with you forever—the Spirit of truth.*" The Greek word for "another," *allos*, from which we get the word *alloy*, means "one exactly like the other." A companion is one who is just like us. There is a similarity of vision, of passion, and of character. There is a similar core to our being. That core is Christ. When we get into trouble, we must be careful concerning the ones we talk to. We need to make sure that those around us are our companions, those of comparable character and parallel purpose.

The reason why we have a company of friends is so that when we tell them about the trouble in our lives, they will go to prayer. And when they start praying, it just doesn't matter anymore. When the friends of Peter and John heard about the threats made against them by the priests, captain of the temple guard, the Sadducees, rulers, elders, and teachers of the law in Jerusalem, *they raised their voices together in prayer to God...* (Acts 4:24). They lifted up their voices to God with one accord about the threat. What was the threat? The threat came because they were preaching about Jesus, and the religious leaders wanted to kill them.

Peter and John were becoming a threat to the religious system, and their preaching exposed the hypocrisy and superficiality of their spiritual lives. When commanded to stop, Peter and John made it clear that they answered to a higher authority and it was to Him that they must be obedient. Their lives were threatened. Through the power of intimidating and hostile words, they were commanded not to speak about Jesus.

A threat is a time-released weapon—against you. The threat is attached to an action that might happen in the future.

Threats seek to lock us into our present and prevent us from the freedom that is ours in Christ. But here's the problem with their threat—and the problem with threats that might come your way. It came too late. The threat came after they had witnessed for themselves God's power.

They knew a man who was now walking—a man who had never taken a step in his life! They had seen for themselves the miraculous power of a loving and forgiving God. He should have never let them see His power. They were *ruined* by it. They had witnessed a power that is greater than earthly power, and they would never be the same. The authorities should have gotten them *before* they witnessed the miracles of Jesus.

The devil should have taken you out *before* you got touched by God. It's too late now. He should have taken you out *before* God delivered you…*before* He healed you…*before* He restored you. The devil should have totally destroyed you *before* God revealed His great love for you and, by the power of His grace, brought you to a place of total restoration. All human and demonic threats are now totally meaningless. They have no bite.

When Peter and John came out of prison, they went to "their own companions." They did not go over there to get pity. They went over there to pray. And, oh my, they did pray.

> *"Sovereign Lord," they said, "you made the heaven and the earth and the sea, and everything in them. You spoke by the Holy Spirit through the mouth of your servant, our father David: 'Why do the nations rage and the peoples plot in vain? The kings of the earth take their stand and the rulers gather together against the Lord and against his Anointed One.' Indeed Herod and Pontius Pilate met together*

with the Gentiles and the people of Israel in this city
to conspire against your holy servant Jesus, whom
you anointed. They did what your power and will
had decided beforehand should happen. Now, Lord,
consider their threats and enable your servants to
speak your word with great boldness. Stretch out
your hand to heal and perform miraculous signs
and wonders through the name of your holy servant
Jesus."

—Acts 4:24-30

They did not pray to be taken out of the trouble, but they prayed for strength to be able to walk through the trouble. These are the kind of friends, the kind of companions you need. O brother, where art thou? You will find them in the house waiting for you to arrive, and when you get there, they are prepared to pray with you and to stand with you in your time of threatening. They will not be overwhelmed by your trouble, but will overwhelm you with their support and encouragement and love. In your hour of need, they will be there.

CHARACTER SKETCH—
FRIENDSHIP

C.S. Lewis and J.R.R. Tolkien

C.S. LEWIS AND J.R.R. TOLKIEN HAVE been elevated to new levels of recognition by the works that have emerged out of Hollywood. Millions have enjoyed the results of their imagination as it has made its way from the book to the screen. The tremendous success of Tolkien's *The Lord of the Rings* and Lewis' *The Lion, The Witch and the Wardrobe,* the first book in the *Chronicles of Narnia,* has been nothing but magical. Not magical in the sense of the *Harry Potter* series but magical in the strength of the script, the charm of the characters, and the vibrancy of the virtues that are portrayed in each story.

It makes one wonder from what brilliance of the soul came such dynamic creativity that makes them transcend the company of other writers. Part of the answer might just be in the friendship that they enjoyed and the influence they had on one another's lives.

What series of circumstances merged together to bring these two men towards each other? They were both professors at

Oxford University and both were authors. Tolkien was a devout Catholic and believer, but Lewis did not share his faith. Prior to C.S. Lewis' conversion, they engaged in many conversations over Christianity as fact or fantasy. One particular evening as they strolled near the University with fellow scholar Hugo Dyson, they had a particularly lively discussion on the subject. This debate over Christianity left such an impact on him that a few days later, Lewis converted to Christianity. The Bible states in Proverbs 27:17: *As iron sharpens iron, so one man sharpens another.* Tolkien's friendship with Lewis had an eternal impact on Lewis' life. Lewis had embraced Christianity and firmly believed that Jesus was indeed the Son of God. This new revelation would strengthen Tolkien and Lewis' friendship and turn Lewis' writing into a new and historical direction. What started as a stroll with friends ended with Lewis making the decision to walk with Christ for the rest of his life.

Only the students of literary history will recognize the name of Dyson, but everyone knows the names of Tolkien and Lewis. The works that created their worldwide reputations are: *The Hobbit* and *The Lord of the Rings* for Tolkien and *The Chronicles of Narnia* and *The Space Trilogy* for Lewis. That evening would be the beginning of a lifelong friendship between Tolkien and Lewis. "...if it hadn't been for the friendship between Tolkien and Lewis, the world would likely never have seen *The Narnia Chronicles* and *The Lord of the Rings*."[1]

"Both Lewis and Tolkien had much in common, as both had been traumatized by the premature death of their mothers and by the horrors of trench warfare in World War I. At age 10, Lewis saw his mother dying of cancer. 'With my mother's death,' said Lewis, 'all that was tranquil and reliable, disappeared from my life.' Tolkien experienced the double loss of both his father at age 3 and his mother at age 12. Tolkien's strong desire for friendship/fellowship, as with Frodo, Sam, Merry & Pippin, came from Tolkien's loss of his three best friends in the trenches. Referring to trench warfare, C.S. Lewis commented: 'Through the winter, weariness and water were our chief enemies. I have gone to sleep marching and woken again and found myself marching still.'… C.S. Lewis commented: 'When I began teaching for the English Faculty, I made two other friends, both Christians (those queer people seemed to pop up on every side) who were later to give me much help in getting over the last steps. They were H.V.D. Dyson and J.R.R. Tolkien. Friendship with the latter marked the breakdown of two old prejudices….'"[2]

Lewis and Tolkien would often fight over the literary value of tales and myths. At first, Lewis saw no value in such fables and sagas, calling them mere lies. Tolkien would retaliate by saying that tales and myths had much more value than what Lewis was seeing. "'No,' Tolkien replied. 'They are not lies.' Tolkien went on to explain that early man, the creators of the great myth cycles, saw the world very differently. To them 'the whole of creation was myth-woven and elf-patterned.' Tolkien went on to argue that man is not ultimately a liar. He may pervert his ideas into lies, but he comes from God, and it is from God that he draws his ultimate ideas. Therefore, Tolkien argued, not only man's abstract thoughts, but also his imaginative inventions, must in some way originate with God, and must in consequence reflect something of eternal truth."[3] It is very clear that the importance and impact of friendship is the key characteristic of the work and life of Tolkien, as illustrated in his most well known work, *The Lord of the Rings*. The tested, but enduring friendship, between Sam and Frodo would inspire millions of readers over the years. It is clear that the friendship that existed between Lewis and Tolkien was mutually beneficial and influenced Tolkien's view of friendship. The bond that developed between them moved them beyond the mere confines of acquaintances. Their lives and words had left a deep imprint upon each other. There was a natural affinity that developed between Lewis and Tolkien because of their passion for the pen, but it was much deeper than that.

Tolkien wrote in his diary, "Friendship with Lewis compensates for much, and besides giving constant pleasure and comfort has done me much good from the contact with a man at once honest, brave, intellectual—a scholar, a poet, and a philosopher—and a lover, at least after a long pilgrimage, of Our Lord."[4]

Early in their relationship, in the mid-1930s Tolkien and Lewis were once again engaged in a thought-provoking conversation that would eventually shape their future works. As they talked about the need to bring their works out of the shadows and on to a larger platform, they made a momentous decision. Lewis made the decision that he would explore space travel in his future works, and Tolkien committed himself to the exploration of time travel. We are all familiar with the success of Lewis' Space Trilogy (*Out of the Silent Planet, Perelandra,* and *That Hideous Strength),* but unfortunately Tolkien never got around to finishing any work on time travel. He was too busy writing an interesting book about hobbits in middle earth.[5]

The friendship that formed between Tolkien and Lewis illustrates the power and necessity of human friendships. No one can deny the power of an imprint of one life on another. We are all the result of the influences of others on our lives. Lewis and Tolkien were deeply encouraged and inspired by their relationship with each other. It was a friendship that was meant to be, and the circle of that friendship has blessed all of us.

> *True friends...face in the same direction, toward common projects, interests, goals.*[6]
>
> — C. S. Lewis

There is a brokenness
of which comes the unbroken,
a shatteredness out of which blooms the
unshatterable.

There is a sorrow
beyond all grief, which leads to joy
and a fragility
out of whose depths emerges strength.

There is a hollow space
too vast for words
through which we pass with each loss,
out of whose darkness we are sanctioned into being.

There is a cry deeper than all sound
whose serrated edges cut the heart
as we break open
to the place inside which is unbreakable
and whole, and learning to sing.

—Author Unknown

CHAPTER FOUR

LIFE IN A CAVE— BROKENNESS

E LIVE IN A TIME when loyalty is at a premium and rather scarce. In the dark corners of the political world, politicians plot and plan for their own benefit as opposed to the benefit of the whole. Success, for many people, is defined within the context of an unholy triad of self-promotion, self-aggrandizement, and self-centeredness. Image is everything and apparently trumps the hidden virtues of loyalty, honesty, and reliability. The ends justify the means and lead to the rise of spin-doctors and media manipulators, treachery and betrayal, and the blurring of ethical lines.

Relationships get lost in the maze of this self-absorbed world that no longer understands the power of loyalty, friendships, and commitment to a common cause.

We were never meant to live in such a narcissistic, egotistical environment—an environment that drains the very life source from our veins. We were born to live in community where the law of that community is "do unto others as you would have them do unto you." There can be no self-fulfillment for us unless we learn to live out our lives in service to others.

Life in a vacuum is a cold, lonely, and futile life. In order to find a new set of models that can inspire us to new heights of commitment and purpose, we return to an ancient cave where we will find a band of misfits and a would-be king. In that ancient cave, we will discover the key that will open up new doors of spiritual opportunity and success—the key of brokenness.

> *David left Gath and escaped to the cave of Adullam. When his brothers and his father's household heard about it, they went down to him there. All those who were in distress or in debt or discontented gathered around him, and he became their leader. About four hundred men were with him. From there David went to Mizpah in Mob and said to the king of Moab, "Would you let my father and mother come and stay with you until I learn what God will do for me?" So he left them with the king of Moab, and they stayed with him as long as David was in the stronghold. But the prophet Gad said to David, "Do not stay in the stronghold. Go into the land of Judah." So David left and went to the forest of Hereth.*
>
> —1 Samuel 22:1-5

THE CAVE

On the borders of the Philistine plain at the base of the Judea mountains, six miles southwest of Bethlehem, there were a number of pits or underground vaults, some nearly square, and all about fifteen or twenty feet deep, with perpendicular sides, in the soft limestone or chalky rocks. These private places in the rock were adapted for concealing refugees or rebels. One of these places was the cave of Adullam, which in Hebrew is translated as, *"It will be a testimony to them."* It will be a testimony, a witness, and a sign to many generations.

What happens in the depth of a cave is more important than what happens on the height of a mountain. It is in the cave times of life that testimonies are forged. You don't establish testimonies on mountaintops. Mountains are places of revelation and spiritual unveiling, but testimonies are chiseled out in the caves of doubt and despair.

Mountains shine bright with the light of His presence while caves are dark where God seems distant and hidden. Mountains show us Who He is and caves reveal who we are. It is in the caves of life that God wants to establish a testimony in your life. Let me tell you a secret about mighty men and women: mighty men know how to find strength in cave times. Mighty men and women of God can go into a cave weak and come out strong.

They can go into a cave confused and come out with understanding. They can go into a cave with doubt and come out with faith. They can go into a cave with "Ichabod" written on their foreheads and come out with the anointing of the Holy Ghost. Mighty men know how to seek out cave times.

WHAT ARE YOU DOING IN A CAVE?

David, how did you get in that cave? What brought you there? David was fleeing and running for his life—from a mad, insane king that he did not understand. All he knew was that he was brought up from a little town called Bethlehem because he could kill giants and play a harp. David possessed dynamic strength and spiritual anointing. His gift and his presence provided peace to the troubled soul of Saul.

But his gifts and anointing were a threat to the soulish Saul, and David was driven out of the palace only to eventually find himself hiding in a cave. Past religious paradigms will always persecute the emerging new order of God in the earth. They will not want to give up their place and position and therefore will force the young man into a cave, rather than give up their throne.

This cave was dark, cold, desolate, lonely, and dreary. What do you suppose David was thinking? Why didn't he go home? Why not go back to Bethlehem? Why not go back to a place where he knew he could dwell in safety? This young boy had more wisdom than to go back to the house of bread. He didn't want to bring trouble to his daddy's house. He was a mature teenager. So, instead of going home, he found a hole in the ground. How did he know where to go? He was a shepherd. He knew every cranny, every nook, every crag, every creek, and every cave in Judah.

The king was angry with him, and he had to hide out somewhere. He had to regroup and figure out what he was going to do. He found the right place in the cave of Adullam. As he entered the cave, he could hear drops of water toward the back coming from the stream that ran behind the cave.

The sun went down. He could hear wolves howling in the distance. He could hear the crickets, grasshoppers, and the sound of locusts. He smelled dust. He was dirty, a little afraid, and pretty confused. As he sat down, he remembered the words of the old prophet Samuel. To the surprise of his whole family, Samuel had anointed him to be a king. What is a king doing in a cave and not living in a castle?

Have you ever felt like that? You came to God and so much of your life was changed. You thought that you would live forever in this spiritual Camelot. From the place of anointing, you went out and killed a giant, and then you were brought before the king. Hey, it doesn't get better than this. Then one day you wake up and find yourself in a world of trouble. Your friends have failed you or you have been afflicted with a severe sickness. You just lost your job and you can't make ends meet. There is nobody there to support you, to encourage you. Welcome to life in the cave.

THE PROCESS OF PAIN

Trouble is a great minister, for trouble knows how to drive you to your knees. David called Adullam "my trouble cave." He met his troubles there, sorted through them with thoughts such as, *I'm in trouble. I don't understand. All I remember is the oil. I remember then after the oil, a few chapters later, that I'm hitting a giant upside the head with a rock, and women are singing,* "David has slain his tens of thousands." There was no better voice than a woman singing, "You're great. You're wonderful. Nobody understands me like you do. David has slain his tens of thousands."

He remembered Goliath. He recalled the harp and the peace that came into that castle when he played for King Saul. David remembered the lion and his sheep. He thought about the bear, and tried to figure out why he was in this cave. David was going to learn that the pathway from aptitude to achievement winds through the valley of preparation. Process is the key to reaching your promised dream. Pain is the process that leads to promise.

David knew how to work a cave. First Samuel 24:3 says, *He came to the sheep pens along the way; a cave was there, and Saul went in to relieve himself. David and his men were far back in the cave.* Saul went in to "relieve himself." Let me show you how David could work a cave. He had trained those 400 men that were with him how to work a cave. Saul and all his men came in the cave after him, and Saul is over there relieving himself, and David and all his men are buried up in cracks in this cave so Saul's men couldn't find them.

There's a secret to turning your cave into a stronghold. Moses knew the secret, for God hid him in the cleft of the rock. When you turn your cave into a stronghold, you can say, "Devil, you drove me in here, but you can't find me. You can search high and low. You've confused my mind, you've gotten me off track, and you've messed up my head, but try to find me now."

David was so slick in the cave that while Saul was over there doing his business, David eased up behind him and just cut the end of his robe off and walked away and Saul didn't even notice him. You've got to know how to work your cave. David knew how to confuse his enemy.

Saul was still his king. He was still his master. And David was never going to harm the king. He could have justified killing Saul, since Saul was trying to kill him, but David refused to even speak an evil word against him. We could all learn from that. He wouldn't even say a bad word, though the man was trying to kill him.

But because God had made Saul his king, his ruler, his monarch, David would not say a bad word against him. Although the man was doing horrible, sinful, ungodly things and David had the opportunity to kill him and put an end to the harassment he had experienced, David refused to even touch him, simply because God had set him on the throne as king. Let me teach you a lesson here: You may not like people who are in authority over you. You might think they're horrible, sinning, filthy people. Don't say a word against them. If God put them in, God will take them out. And if you take them out, God will take you out.

God sets up, and God takes down. David could have killed Saul, who had come in that cave to kill him. But David cut off the end of Saul's robe and shouted, "Saul, King Saul!"

"David, is that you? David, is that… you…? What do you have in your hand? What is that?"

"It's your robe," David replied. "I could have killed you, but I know how to work my cave. You came to kill me but you couldn't find me."

Let me tell you what I love to do. I love to mess with the enemy's head. Paul says in the New Testament books of Ephesians and 1 Corinthians, "Don't be ignorant of the devil's devices. Outwit him." (See 2 Corinthians 2:11; Ephesians 6:11.) When he tries to find you, just be buried in the name…buried in the blood.

Hebrews 11 is often referred to as the Hall of Faith. Verses 37 and 38 of that chapter tell us that these great men and women of faith …*were stoned; they were sawed in two; they were put to death by the sword. They went about in sheepskins and goatskins, destitute, persecuted and mistreated—the world was not worthy of them. They wandered in deserts and mountains, **and in caves and holes in the ground*** (emphasis added). So don't feel strange when you find yourself in a cave.

Let's look at 1 Samuel 23:29, *And David went up from there and lived in the strongholds* [or caves] *of En Gedi.* David so learned how to work his caves that he became so familiar with the cave life that he chose to live there. He didn't have to, and you'll find out that at the peak of his kingdom, he had 329,000 soldiers, but there was a day in his life that he still chose to go get in a cave. Now he doesn't live in that cave, but he chooses to go to it. Why?

David chose to go to the cave because he knew how to find strength in the caves of his life. He had learned as you and I must learn that character is forged in the firestorms of life and virtue is etched into your life in the dark places. Inspired by the caves of his own life, St. John of the Cross wrote these words:

> *O guiding light!*
> *O night more lovely than the dawn!*
> *O night that has united*
> *The Lover with His beloved*
> *Transforming the beloved in her Lover.*

SONGS IN THE CAVE

It is in the cave of Adullam that David wrote one of his greatest Psalms. Look at Psalm 142:1: *I cry aloud to the Lord.* Can you see Jesse's face as he walks into the cave and hears his son singing this song? *I lift up my voice to the Lord for mercy. I pour out my complaint before him; before him I tell my trouble. When my spirit grows faint within me, it is you who know my way. In the path where I walk men have hidden a snare for me. Look to my right and see...* (vv. 1-4).

The pitch of pain was dribbling out of the soul of the man who longed for peace and acceptance and relief. Have you ever felt lonely in your life? *Look to my right and see; no one is concerned for me. I have no refuge; no one cares for my life. I cry to you, O Lord; I say, "You are my refuge, my portion in the land of the living." Listen to my cry, for I am in desperate need* (vv. 4-6).

These are strange words. *Rescue me from those who pursue me, for they are too strong for me. Set me free from my prison that I may praise your name. Then the righteous will gather about me because of your goodness to me* (vv. 6,7).

And when he got to the part that says, "the righteous will gather about me," he looked up, and about five or ten men with disheveled hair, undone…thieves…robbers…men who have no direction for their lives began to track their way down that cave looking at him, saying, "Here we come." What? Is this his divine help? These are not the people he expected. He is down, deep in the cave, and here came a congregation, and it was not the congregation that the preacher wanted to see. It was a generation of misfits, druggies, prostitutes, and dropouts. David had to be thinking, *Where are the doctors, bankers, and lawyers, professional athletes, movie stars, and other influential folk? Who are these guys? Why didn't these guys shave before they came to this cave?*

A 3-D ARMY—DISTRESSED, DISCONTENTED, AND IN DEBT

The Bible describes them as a 3-D army: in distress, discontented, and in debt. Welcome to David's church. This is David's first army: in distress. The word *distress* in this context means that these people were in a squeeze. They were in debt. They had a creditor that was lording over them. They owed more than they could pay. They were discontented. The word *discontented* here means they were "bitter in their souls." They had broken relationships behind them. They had their issues. All they knew was that this man who had killed Goliath was in a hole in the ground somewhere, and they were determined to find him, knowing that since David was broken, he would be able to understand them.

Let me tell you a secret. I never want to hear a preacher who hasn't walked through a valley. I don't ever want to hear a preacher who hasn't been broken. I will not listen to a preacher who has never experienced debt, distress, and discontent. He doesn't have anything to say to me. Experience in life should bring a certain compassion for others and a wisdom that is birthed in the fire of trials and troubles.

During the course of his life, David had been a shepherd, a warrior and, finally, he was a king. At this time in his life, he didn't need shepherds or kings—he needed warriors. He needed people who understood how to fight—people who, not knowing what else to do, would just grab a sword and swing. This is a study in brokenness. Some people have not had enough trouble in their lives.

The reason why you can't cry in the presence of God is that you haven't had enough brokenness. David knew brokenness intimately. This man was supposed to be a king! That's why he could get in a cave and write a psalm that said, *Set me free from my prison, that I may praise your name.* And then he just confessed, *Then the righteous will gather about me because of your goodness to me* (Psalm 142:7). Before he knew it, 400 people had come into the cave to join him.

You aren't the only one who has ever been in trouble. In the place of trouble, relationships are formed that last for a lifetime. Brokenness and weakness have a certain aroma that attracts others with the same scent. When you get in relationships with other people and realize that they have survived a great deal of sorrow in their lives, suddenly a connection is formed.

I know what it is to be broken…I know what it is to be confused…I know what it is to make mistakes. I know what it is to be misunderstood…I know what it is to be abused…I know what it is to live through broken relationships, not really knowing what happened. God's trying to tell us something: Our strength will be found in union with other people who have tracked through the troubles of life.

DAVID'S FIRST ARMY

Watch what David does with these people. First Chronicles 12:1,2 says, *These were the men who came to David at Ziklag, while he was banished from the presence of Saul son of Kish (they were among the warriors who helped him in battle; they were armed with bows and were able to shoot arrows or to sling stones right-handed or left-handed; they were kinsmen of Saul from the tribe of Benjamin).*

They said, "This brother's so bad, we're going to him." Some of those 400 people left Saul and came to David, and a shift began to take place in Israel. These warriors sensed that something was happening, and they were going to cast their lot with the man in the cave.

This was David's first army. Now watch this: David took time to take broken people who had broken lives. They were hurt, confused and misunderstood, in distress, discontent, and in debt, and I think David might have said, "I accept you as you are. I am going to teach you how to war for your life. I'm going to teach you how to use the name of the coming Messiah. And when the name of our Messiah doesn't work, I'm going to teach you how to put the Word of God out there. If the Word won't work, then we're going to fast, and if fasting doesn't work, we're going to have united prayer. If united prayer doesn't work, then we're going to intercede."

"But some way, somehow, we're going to keep slinging stones, right hand, left hand, right hand, left hand, right hand, left hand, until we win this war!" These men could split a hair at 100 yards with a rock. They could stretch a hair between two sticks in the ground, throw a rock from 100 yards, and split the hair in two. These men knew what they were doing. But they hadn't been like that all along. When they first came to David, they were a messed up group of misfits who had decided that life with him was much better than life in the palace. Good things begin in obscure places.

Jesus was not born at the best hospital in town. He was born in a barn, and when He went in search of companions—those who would stand *next to* Him—He chose a man named Simon Peter, who would pull out a sword if he had to, to fight for his Savior. Jesus didn't go to the biggest office building in town and look for the top executives to join him. He went to the seashore and found the man that cursed the most and smelled the worst, and I imagine He told him: "You're the man I'm looking for. You have tenacity in you. You have a warrior spirit in you. They call you Simon, but you shall be called a rock!"

> *But God chose the foolish things of the world to shame the wise; God chose the weak things of the world to shame the strong. He chose the lowly things of this world and the despised things—and the things that are not—to nullify the things that are, so that no one may boast before him.*
> —1 Corinthians 1:27-29

The ways of God are quite different than the ways of man. The kingdoms of this world are built on the foundations of the educated, the wealthy, the powerful and the privileged. The kingdom of God is built upon the weak, the poor, the unlearned and the disenfranchised so that all men will give glory to God. It is the kingdom of Saul versus the kingdom of David.

MORE SORROW, MORE PAIN, AND MORE VICTORY

These men found David in a hole in the ground. He knew he was hurting and sick, but he also knew he loved God with all his heart. He needed to be around 400 more people like himself who understood him. Look what happens with these guys. First Samuel 30:1 says, *David and his men reached Ziklag on the third day.* They had just returned from Achish where they were working with the Philistines. David was so sly at one point that he took his whole army, which had grown from 400 to 600 men, and joined them with the Philistines. How could he have done that? David slipped right into the Philistine army and worked for them just to keep his brothers from being killed. I don't know about you, but I think that's awesome!

I believe the strongest voice that's going to be heard in this land in the last day is going to be the church's voice. We had better quit saying Jesus is the answer, and start telling *why* He's the answer. It's easy to say He's the answer. It's also easy to say Mohammed is the answer. But why is Jesus the answer and Mohammed not the answer? That answer must be manifested, not by the supercilious, scornful voices of religion, but manifested by a company of men and women who know their God and have experienced His supernatural power in their lives.

In 1 Samuel 29:7, Achish sends David back to Ziklag. Achish gave David that city. Now, watch what happens when David gets back (30:1-4), *Now the Amalekites had raided the Negev and Ziklag. They had attacked Ziklag and burned it, and had taken captive the women and all who were in it, both young and old. They killed none of them, but carried them off as they went on their way. When David and his men came to Ziklag, they found it destroyed by fire and their wives and sons and daughters taken captive. So David and his men wept aloud until they had no strength left to weep.*

How much must one suffer? Who can heal the pain of this heart? Can you see them just fall apart, look at David, and say: "David, look what you did." They got on David. Verse 6 says, *the men were talking of stoning him.* And David said to them "Hey, guys, hold it a second." The Bible says he had to encourage his own self. Before you can help someone else, you had better take care of yourself. When your friend becomes your foe, you're in trouble. When your friend misunderstands you and turns on you, you're in trouble. David believed he had relationship with these men. He talked to them and said, "Wait a minute, fellows," and he won back their hearts.

This is powerful. He said, "Listen, I'm going to pray." (See vv. 7 and 8.) God said to go and *overtake them and succeed in the rescue* (v. 8). Watch what happens. Essentially David said, "All six hundred of you, big burly, fighting men, follow me. We're going to get what the devil took from us, and we're going to retrieve everything we lost." That's passion! They responded by agreeing to go with David. Now, as they went, two hundred of the six hundred men couldn't make it. The Bible says they were *too exhausted to cross the ravine* (v. 10). Some folks can't hang with you. It happens. Some people just can't hang. You start pursuing, you start praying, you say, "We're going on a thirty-day fast, come on, get with it," and watch who hangs. So David and the 400 go and recover all.

First Chronicles 12:18 tells us that these mighty men who followed David, along with Amasai, chief of the Thirty, cried, "*Success! Success to* [King David] *and success to those who help you, for your God will help you.*" I don't know what beat they used, but they sang, "Success to King David!" Can you hear these 400 men roaring? They met a young man on the way who betrayed them to the Amalekites, so David and his men threatened him and got him to tell them where their wives and children were. They saw the Amalekites who had just raided their city and taken their wives and children, and said, "There they are." Can you just picture David in your mind? I can just see him. They went in there, and 1 Samuel 30:17 says, *David fought them from dusk until the evening of the next day and none of them got away, except four hundred young men who rode off on camels and fled.* No member of David's army was lost. There was a field full of bodies, and David's 400 men screamed, "Success, success!" David told them to gather their wives and children and go home.

So they started to walk off, and verses 18 and 19 say, *David recovered everything the Amalekites had taken, including his two wives. Nothing was missing: young or old, boy or girl, plunder or anything else they had taken. David brought everything back. He took all the flocks and herds, and his men drove them ahead of the other livestock, saying, "This is David's plunder."* He took all their jewelry, their weapons, their food, and their money. They messed with the wrong brothers! David and 400 bloody, fighting men started tracking their way back home. Guess who they meet on their way? The 200 men who said, "We can't hang."

They saluted David saying, "Success!" David's men started bickering, saying these 200 shouldn't get any of the spoil because they hadn't fought. They let them know in no uncertain terms that they could get their wives and families and go live somewhere else. They didn't want them to live in Ziklag any more. They felt forsaken by the 200.

Guess what David did? *David replied, "No, my brothers, you must not do that with what the Lord has given us. He has protected us and handed over to us the forces that came against us. Who will listen to what you say? The share of the man who stayed with the supplies is to be the same as that of him who went down to the battle. All will share alike." David made this a statute and ordinance for Israel from that day to this* (1 Samuel 30:23-25).

In other words, David said, "Hold it, guys! Do you think you won that war? Great leaders rise in the midst of challenging situations. It will take wisdom to break this controversy and bring peace back to the situation. You think it was your strength that won the war? You think that was you who swung that sword and cut that man's head off? You think you're so bad? The Lord did that for you. Give these men what belongs to them. You boys are coming home with us." There are times when some of us are weak and we can't make it! All personal victory should become a corporate celebration.

First Samuel 22:5 says that the prophet of Gad was in the cave, telling David not to stay in the cave because he had work to do. Now, at the end of the chapter, someone else shows up. In verse 20 it says that Abiathar was there. Abiathar was a priest. He was the last one in the cave. He was the last one home. You know what that meant? Now David was complete. He had warriors, he had a prophet, and now he had a priest. A priest is symbolic of worship, incense, and offering.

When David saw Abiathar walk through the mouth of that cave, I can tell you what happened to his heart. It started pounding hard. David had to ask him what he was doing there. Saul had ordered that all the priests be killed. David must have thought, *I knew it. I knew he was going to do it.* He must have thought to himself, *I knew you were going to come to me.* David had to be moved to the point of tears, because now he knew God was on his side.

Remember in the first few verses where he had asked, *"Would you let my father and mother come and stay with you until I learn what God will do for me?"* (v. 3). When Abiathar walked in, he knew. He must have looked at Gad and said, "Don't worry, brother, we aren't staying any longer. We're coming out, and we're going to take care of business."

There's a time to be in the cave and there is a time to come out of the cave. The God who gave you grace and comfort in the cave will now give you favor and blessing as you emerge out of the cave into the new place that has been designed for you. There comes a time when the people of God will become manifest to the world—put on display by the Spirit of God. They will take their place in the marketplace, and their wisdom will be heard in the streets. All men will bow to the wisdom and might of our great God who has prepared such an awesome people.

CHARACTER SKETCH— BROKENNESS

Watchman Nee

WATCHMAN NEE, BORN NÍ TUÒSHĒNG in 1903, became a Christian in 1920 at the age of 17. His original name was Shu-Tsu, but was changed to To-Sheng which means the sound of a watchman alerting others to danger. "He changed his name to Watchman Nee because he saw it as someone that stayed up in the middle of the night to awaken men of the coming of Christ."[1] Early in his life, it was clear that Watchman Nee was destined for something special because of his commitment to the cause of Christ in China. While others were pursuing other things in life, Nee had only one passionate purpose—to build his life around the purposes of God. Nee had an extraordinary passion for the Scriptures and an exceptional compassion for God's people.

He was devoted to the study of the Scriptures and learning as much as he could. In his pursuit of spiritual knowledge, Nee had collected over 3,000 Christian books. Nee avidly read his Bible, and as his spiritual hunger continued to grow, he eventually entered Dora Yu's Bible Institute in Shanghai.

In 1928, Watchman Nee established the Shanghai Gospel Bookroom, which became the center for his developing ministry. It was through SGB that he published his own books and from time to time the works of other authors. One of the men that he published was T. Austin Sparks. Watchman Nee had traveled to Honor Oak Christian Fellowship Centre in London to be mentored by Sparks. When comparing the writings of Sparks and Nee, the impact that Sparks had on the young Nee becomes clear. Nee's passion for the centrality of Christ grew out of his friendship with Sparks, who had written several books on the subject and was passionate for the glory of Christ.

As one tracks the life of Watchman Nee, it becomes clear that two passions began to develop in his life. These passions are manifested in the life that he lived and in the words that he wrote. His primary passion, as we have already indicated, was that God's people understand the message and the work of Christ. Secondly, he was committed to planting and establishing churches throughout China. Nee traveled with a band of other Christians declaring the message of Jesus Christ. Once he started bringing people to Christ, he exchanged his role as an evangelist for the role of a teacher. It was as a teacher of the Word that Watchman Nee found his most powerful gift. His deep, personal knowledge and experience of Christ coupled with the emerging revelation of God's purpose for the church gave rise to a plethora of books that he would write. Nee was driven to discover "normal" Christianity as experienced by the primitive church in the book of Acts. This passion led to the writing of his most well-known book, *The Normal Christian Life* and a lesser-known book, *The Normal Christian Church Life.*

Nee was committed to the task of spreading the Gospel throughout China. As the message of Christ was spread through meetings in people's homes and the church grew, he had to find a place that would hold the burgeoning gatherings. Little Flock became the name of these house churches that were springing up all over China. It was in these groups that Nee taught the truths that became popular through the books that he wrote. Brokenness became a constant theme in the preaching of Nee. Like his mentor, T. Austin Sparks, Nee believed that man could not be effective as a witness for Christ unless the vessel had been broken. Through the process of brokenness, the sweet aroma of Christ would emanate from Christ's messengers.

The establishment of the church in these groups that were living out the message of Christ in their homes would be able to survive the coming onslaught of communism because they had been prepared by Nee. Life in the cave would make them strong for the coming oppression.

"The more than six hundred local churches raised up in China through the ministry of Watchman Nee before the communist revolution have had an undisputed impact on the formation of the Christian church in China."[2]

Even before the coming persecution of the communist, Nee would suffer greatly. "Ill health was another source of suffering that frequently struck Nee. Tuberculosis, chronic stomach disorder, angina pectoris (heart ailment) were some of the largest obstacles of Nee's health."[3]

Mao-Tse Tung and his army of radical communists finally won their last battle and took control of China in 1949. Because Watchman Nee would not bend his knee to the new government during the Cultural Revolution, he was arrested and falsely condemned. He could not pledge allegiance to the new government. His life was already pledged to Another. In 1952 he was arrested and subjected to cruel punishment and psychological reeducation. Finally he was taken to trial in 1956, and he was sentenced to fifteen years in prison. That sentence was extended, and twenty years after the initial sentence, Watchman Nee died a martyr's death in prison at the age of sixty-nine. "He left a piece of paper under his pillow, which had several lines of big words written in a shaking hand: 'Christ Is the Son of God who died for the redemption of sinners and resurrected after three days. This is the greatest truth in the universe. I die because of my belief in Christ.'"[4]

Like his Master, Watchman Nee endured persecution and suffered much for the cause of His Lord. As he walked through the valley of suffering, Nee learned much about the ways of the Lord, and during those times of suffering, he did not waver because of the constant supply of grace flooding into his battered soul.

"Watchman Nee's writings on matters of the individual Christian life have been a source of inspiration to Christians throughout the world, though his writings on the local churches—which he considered to be central to his ministry—have been largely ignored by mainstream Christianity."[5] Another well-known book by Nee was *Release of the Spirit.* In this classic book on brokenness, Nee describes the sweet aroma that ascends from a life that is broken. In the preface to the book he writes, "Beloved, we are convinced that this matter of true brokenness before the Lord is the great need of this closing hour. One has well said that the Lord uses for His glory those servants who are most perfectly broken. Is not this what Isaiah meant when he exclaimed: 'the lame that take the prey!' Surely when the beautiful alabaster box has received the breaking blow, the fragrance of the perfume is released to fill the house with refreshing and quickening."[6]

When David was overcome by the people and cares of his life, he escaped to a place that was familiar to him. A place of refuge. A place where he spent many nights as a young shepherd boy. Now as a battle-worn warrior, carrying the weight of a nation and only steps ahead of death, it would again be his refuge. He knew this place. He had dreamed here. Seen visions here. It was here in the cave where he had written songs and poems and poured out his heart and heard God's voice. Here is where his courage, strength, and boldness were birthed to kill the lion, bear, and Goliath.

Only this time David would not be alone. Other men came. Those who were in distress, in debt, and discontented gathered around him in the cave. Rejected and overcome with life, they too were searching for a refuge. A place where they could find their honor, strength, and understanding and bare their souls without judgment.

Something happened in the cave; for later they were referred to as mighty men.

—Jake Jones

CHAPTER FIVE

FACING THE BATTLE—COURAGE

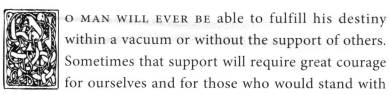O MAN WILL EVER BE able to fulfill his destiny within a vacuum or without the support of others. Sometimes that support will require great courage for ourselves and for those who would stand with us. The road to destiny will often take us through treacherous terrains and perilous places. It is not a journey for wimps and weasels. David was on a journey that would eventually lead to a throne where he would become king of Israel. But before he arrived at his destiny, he was forced to hide in caves and fight his enemies.

This was not a journey he could succeed at by himself. He just wouldn't survive alone. So as he waited in a cave, God would bring him people who would courageously stand with him. They may not have been the kind of people he would have chosen. They rarely are. Those who walk where others will not are willing to give up the secure places for a while because they have seen what others cannot see.

When these people joined David in the wilderness they won his admiration, and in the coming days their actions would win his heart.

THREE MIGHTY MEN AND THEIR KING

*These are the names of the mighty men whom David had: Josheb-basshebeth a Tahchemonite, chief of the captains; the same was **Adino** the Eznite, against eight hundred slain at one time. And after him was **Eleazar** the son of Dodai the son of an Ahohite, one of the three mighty men with David, when they defied the Philistines that were there gathered together to battle, and the men of Israel were gone away. He arose, and smote the Philistines until his hand was weary, and his hand clave unto the sword; and Jehovah wrought a great victory that day; and the people returned after him only to take spoil. And after him was **Shammah** the son of Agee a Hararite. And the Philistines were gathered together into a troop, where was a plot of ground full of lentils; and the people fled from the Philistines. But he stood in the midst of the plot, and defended it, and slew the Philistines; and Jehovah wrought a great victory.*

—2 Samuel 23:8-12 ASV, emphasis added

Among all the people who joined David in the cave there were three who stood out. These warriors were no rookies or novices.

They had faced the enemy—thousands of enemies—and had overcome. They had stared death in the face and had not faltered. They had prevailed in the face of overwhelming odds. Courage like this is not a gift you can buy or an art you can learn. Either you have it or you don't. These three men had it. These men had the heart of their leader, David. They knew what he was thinking before he spoke it. They loved God exactly as David loved God. They loved to fight like David loved to fight. These men were gutsy and gifted. They were David's most loyal and trusted men, and they followed him anywhere he decided to go.

Their steps were found in the footprints of David, and their bedrolls were as close to him as they could possibly get them. David entrusted his future into the hands of these men, for they had proved their love for him and were committed to his cause, his purpose, and his future.

ADINO THE EZNITE—FIGHT FOR WHAT BELONGS TO YOU

Adino is the son of Zabdeal, who was a priest whose name means, "I'm a gift of God." Adino's name means, "Given to pleasure or to be pleasant, voluptuous" and also means "dweller among the people; or to whom the people turn." Adino was identified as the chief of the three. There is something unique about him that makes him stand out among the other warriors. I find it very interesting that at the head of David's list, he would have this handsome, young gentleman, who may have been passionate about women just as David was and who also attracted the heart of the people. He was the chief of everybody. He was "the man." He sat in the captain's chair. He was handsome, strong, and a natural leader, but in spite of all of his natural ability and charisma, he chose to submit his life to another. He chose to submit his will and destiny to the will and destiny of David. A man like Adino would not submit his life to just any man, but David had won his heart.

Adino was from the tribe of Korahites. Tachmonite, as it reads here, is better translated in the Hebrew as the Hacmonite, from the line of Korah. Korah was a descendant of Levi, from which we get the Levitical priesthood—the tribe of Levi. The Korahites were singers. The sons of Korah wrote the twelfth psalm. They also wrote Psalms 42 through 49 and Psalms 84, 85, 87, and 88. Adino is a descendant of a company of worshippers whose literary work is recorded in the Jewish scriptures. They wrote this classic song of worship:

> *To the chief Musician upon Gittith, A Psalm for the sons of Korah:*
>
> *How amiable are thy tabernacles, O Lord of hosts! My soul longeth, yea, even fainteth for the courts of the Lord: my heart and my flesh crieth out for the living God. Yea, the sparrow hath found an house, and the swallow a nest for herself, where she may lay her young, even thine altars, O Lord of hosts, my King, and my God. Blessed are they that dwell in thy house: they will be still praising thee. Selah. Blessed is the man whose strength is in thee; in whose heart are the ways of them. Who passing through the valley of Baca make it a well; the rain also filleth the pools. They go from strength to strength, every one of them in Zion appeareth before God. O Lord God of hosts, hear my prayer: give ear, O God of Jacob. Selah. Behold, O God our shield, and look upon the face of thine anointed. For a day in thy courts is better than a thousand. I had rather be a doorkeeper*

*in the house of my God, than to dwell in the tents of
wickedness. For the Lord God is a sun and shield: the
Lord will give grace and glory: no good thing will he
withhold from them that walk uprightly. O Lord of
hosts, blessed is the man that trusteth in thee.*
—Psalm 84, KJV

From the power and inspiration of the Korahites came one
who would stand alongside David and serve him in his journey
to the throne.

In 1 Chronicles 27:2, the Bible says of Adino that he was
the commander in chief of the first army of the first month.
In other words, on the first month of every year, Adino took
24,000 men, and they protected David's kingdom. That was very
important, because what David wanted to do in the first month
of every year was to establish that he was still the "mightiest"
king on the earth. In order to establish his preeminence, he
chose the most ruthless of them all, Adino. He put him over
24,000 men and they would rout any enemy that would come
close to them. In 2 Samuel 23:8, we discover that he was the
chief of the captains, and that he killed eight hundred men at
one time.

The spear that Adino used was deadly because you could kill
with the spear in both directions. It was pointed and dangerous
on both ends. The spear was just as bad coming back at you as it
was coming toward you. But the most amazing thing about the
spear was that the spear weighed about two hundred pounds.
So Adino may have been slim but he was awfully strong.

The Bible does not say what happened this day. It just says
"in one encounter." In other words, it almost leaves the impres-
sion that at "one time" Adino got mad and killed 800 men in

one fight. Now, that's a bad, mean brother. He is dangerous just holding that spear, much less being able to swing it with such velocity that he could kill people all day long. It took much skill and much practice to use the spear.

Joel 3:9,10 says, *Proclaim ye this among the Gentiles; Prepare war, wake up the mighty men, let all the men of war draw near; let them come up: Beat your plowshares into swords, and your pruning hooks into spears: let the weak say, I am strong* (KJV). This is a prophecy concerning the end of days. The prophet then talks about plowshares and pruning hooks. What are these used for?

Plowshares are used for plowing fields and pruning hooks are used for trimming. When you use these instruments, you're just maintaining your field, your garden. They are instruments used for taking care of what belongs to you. The prophet is saying that there will come a time when you will put aside the instruments that were once used to take care of what belongs to you, and you will turn them into instruments to deal with your enemies. There is a time for farming and there is a time for fighting. Now is the time for fighting. It is not a time for weakness but for strength. It is a time for leaving the fields and going toward the battlefield. You just might lose your field if you are not willing to fight for what is yours.

Quit saying, "I am weak!" If Adino had walked into David's cave saying, "I am weak," David would have said, "Find another hole in the ground. I don't have time for maintaining weak brothers." What the Lord is saying to us is that we need to quit maintaining and start advancing. The Lord is saying it's time for you to beat your pruning hooks into spears. You need to learn how to use your spear so that you can fight frontward and backward.

If the devil comes behind you or in front of you, stab him with the spear. God has a weapon for you uniquely designed in a way that will protect your rear and your front—spiritual weapons that will bring down every evil force that is seeking to bring you down. Now is the time to hand in your farm utensils and take up the sword and fight for what belongs to you. It is not enough to simply "hold on." It is a time to "move on."

ELEAZAR—THE LOYAL ONE

The second man among David's mighty men was Eleazar the son of Dodai the Ahohite. Jewish tradition tells us that Dodai was a brother of Jesse, and if this is true then Eleazar was David's cousin. As one of the three mighty men, he was with David when they taunted the Philistines gathered for battle. Eleazar stood strong in the battle, fighting the Philistines one after another. Wave upon wave of Philistines came at him and they all died by his sword. He had gripped his sword for so long that his hand grew tired and froze to the sword. The Lord brought about a great victory that day, according to the Bible.

Eleazar means "the court of God," or "God is my helper; the help of God." Dodai's name means, "I am fond of making love." It is interesting that David attracted men who had a fiery passion for women. One thing I find interesting about God is that He does not choose as we would choose. Along with David, these men had a weakness for women. When you find yourself in a cave and your enemies want to kill you, it is better to have someone with you who can identify with your weakness and give you support.

Great relationships are bonded and formed in places of weakness. David and his men had great strengths, but they identified best at their points of weakness. It is important to have people in our lives who know what we are going through and can identify with our weaknesses so they can cover us while God works to heal us. We don't need super-spiritual, pride-filled people who will look down on us in our weaknesses. We need caring and understanding people who will extend a hand of support to us.

Eleazar was a descendent of Ahoa; therefore, he was an Ahohite. *Ahoa* means "I belong to the brotherhood." That tells me that Eleazar was raised to believe in relationships. There is power in a name, and Eleazar was a son of the brotherhood. When you name your child, you pronounce his destiny. Eleazar believed in the power of brothers—the power of relationships—and he sought out people with whom he could bond.

First Chronicles 27 records that Dodai, the father of Eleazar was also a mighty man and that he was the commander of 24,000 in the second month. So when the second month came around, David called on Dodai. "Now you cover us for a month, you and your 24,000." What is so interesting about this is the father and son thing. What is more interesting is that the son chosen to be with David was not Dodai. It is a generational thing.

God's purpose is to extend His purpose and power through the generations and that there be an increase in power and purpose in the succeeding generations. Eleazar was able to exceed all that his father had accomplished.

It is interesting to note that Ahoa was the grandson of Benjamin, placing Eleazar in the line of Benjamin. Let me tell you about Benjamin. He's the youngest of the twelve tribes. Benjamin's name means, "I'm a ravenous wolf." He might be the youngest, but he is the meanest.

Every man in the line of Benjamin was very aggressive in what they did, even Saul (in the Old Testament). A wolf can devour seven times its weight in food, and this belligerent characteristic was evident in all the men from the line of Benjamin. Now, here is Eleazar. What is in this man's blood that makes him take a sword and kill all day long until his hand freezes to his weapon? What is in him? His father is in him, and not only his father, but his grandfather is in him and his great-grandfather and his great-great-grandfather. And then Benjamin is living in Eleazar, so that when Eleazar takes the sword, he just does what is in his blood.

My three brothers and I are all different, until we get mad. Then we're all the same. Do you understand what I'm telling you? It's the same thing with you and your family. Think about it. Look at your brothers and sisters. You may all be different, but when someone attacks the family, you all unite against them, no matter what your gift or your personality. Eleazar just got up one day with his sword and decided to kill Philistines all day until his hand actually froze to the sword.

Here are three characteristics of Eleazar. Number one, he was *loyal*. Loyalty. Don't forget the word loyalty, because that's the most important word in this chapter. Loyalty. The first key to commitment is a loyalty and faithfulness that goes beyond all personal feelings. I read recently that the 28th president of the United States, Woodrow Wilson, once declared that loyalty means nothing unless it has at its heart the absolute principle of self-sacrifice.

Loyalty is a faithfulness that is steadfast in the face of any temptation to renounce, desert, or betray. It is the powerful combination of absolute devotion, tender attachment, and authentic love. Someone said that loyalty is the measuring stick of love. And, without a doubt, Eleazar was loyal to David. His devotion, attachment, and love were unquestionable.

Number two is the fact that Eleazar was *courageous.* When everyone else left, he stood alone, committed to the cause regardless of the cost. Someone said that a man with courage is a majority. Number three, Eleazar was *committed to what he believed.* His hand froze to the sword. He was from the tribe of Benjamin. It was easy for him to stand and fight all day long because that's who he was. It was in his blood. He was loyal, courageous, and committed. Where have all the good men gone? Where are those who know the power of loyalty, the strength of courage, and the joy of commitment?

We live in a day when we must see the restoration of a new generation of men and women who have entered into the company of the loyal, the courageous, and the committed.

SHAMMAH—THE MAN OF THE PRESENCE

The last of these three is Shammah the son of Agee the Hararite. The writer of 2 Samuel records this story about his valor in the days of the wars between the Jews and the Philistines. When the Philistines had banded together at a place where there was a field full of lentils (beans), Israel's troops fled in fear from them. Not Shammah. He took his stand in the middle of the field. He defended it and struck the Philistines down, and the Lord brought about a great victory. (See 2 Samuel 23:11,12.) When others were running from the enemy, Shammah stood his ground and defeated the enemy.

His name means "obedience." His father's name is Agee. His name means "I'm a fugitive—can't find a home." They were Hararites, which means "we dwell in the mountain," or "give me my mountain." The most interesting thing about Shammah is his relationship with his father. In 1 Chronicles 11:34,

Jonathan, his son, was also listed as one of the mighty men. This was another father-and-son team.

I can proudly say that I believe I belong to the mighty men of God, and I believe my son is right in the cave with me. And I encourage you fathers not to give up on your sons. I believe in the power of fathers and sons. It is the enemy's desire to take our children from us, but it is the desire of the Father to restore the sons to the fathers.

Shammah was from the clan of Caleb. Caleb's son Haran was his descendant. Hararites are the descendants of Caleb, and Caleb is a descendant of the tribe of Judah. They're mountaineers. Shammah was a little possessive. He called it his mountain. Shammah was a man of the mountain, the place of the presence, the place of security, and the place of revelation. It will take men of the mountain to be able to win battles in the valley. Mountains are not for our dwelling—they are for our restoration, healing, and instruction so that we can return to the valley.

Every mountain experience will bring you to a place of trouble and opportunity in the valley. Mountain experiences are great, but mountain experiences will prepare you to succeed in the day of trouble. When Jesus descended from the Mount of Transfiguration, He encountered His disciples battling demons, and not doing a very good job. From the mountain of revelation, Jesus came to the valley to rescue His disciples and heal this demon-possessed man. Shammah found his strength in the mountain places. Where do you find your strength?

FOR THE LOVE OF A BROTHER

During harvest time, three of the thirty chief men came down to David at the cave of Adullam (the

*place of testimony), while a band of Philistines was
encamped in the Valley of Rephaim. At that time,
David was in the stronghold, and the Philistine
garrison was at Bethlehem. David longed for water
and said, "Oh, that someone would get me a drink
of water from the well near the gate of Bethlehem!"
So the three mighty men broke through the Philistine
lines, drew water from the well near the gate of
Bethlehem, and carried it back to David. But he
refused to drink it; instead, he poured it out before
the Lord. "Far be it from me, O LORD, to do this!"
he said. "Is it not the blood of men who went at the
risk of their lives?" And David would not drink it.
Such were the exploits of the three mighty men.*

—2 Samuel 23:13-17

Three mighty men came down to the cave of Adullam. We just met these men. They are Eleazar from the tribe of Benjamin, Adino from the tribe of Levi, and Shammah from Judah. As they enter the cave, you can hear the crickets and the water running. The sun is descending into the horizon. Everybody is in there. There are campfires built in different places in the cave. Uriah is on one side, some other guys on the other side, and some are in the back.

Just as the sun dips into the distant horizon, in walks Eleazar, Adino, and Shammah. They walk in together. As they walk in, everybody turns in their direction because these are the three mightiest men in the army of David. The chatter stops as soon as they enter the cave.

Adino, with his sensual self, (pretty boy), being from the Levitical priesthood, is always one who's hopping and bopping and looking for a battle. He always wants to write a song about everything because his blood says, "I'm going to sing! I'll sing my way out of this trouble." That's Adino—he's a fighter and a worshipper. He's got the looks and everything, but more than that, he likes to sing and he loves to fight. You make Adino mad, and he'll just go kill 800 people in one day!

Then we have Eleazar, from the tribe of Benjamin. When I picture Eleazar in my mind, he should have red hair. Have you ever seen a redheaded kid who's nervous? It's like they have a lot of fire—so much fire that their hair is red, and they have little sweat beads sliding down their foreheads. You go to their room, and it's all messed up. You might get hit if you come close to the door, because this guy is a ravenous wolf. He's always moving. He's never still, and even when he is still, he's still moving, ready for the next battle, and he has this mischievous look in his eyes. He looks almost crazy. He's constantly thinking, *I've got to do something!* This is Eleazar. It's not a problem for him to hold a sword all day. He was made for battle!

And here is Shammah from the tribe of Judah. Everybody thinks *Judah* means "praise," but it doesn't only mean praise, it means "loud." He's loud! You know when Shammah is around.

So they walk in, and some of the men ask them, "Hey, guys, what's happening?" And these three say, "The Philistines are building a garrison around Bethlehem." A garrison is a troop. It's not the whole army of the Philistines, but a troop around the city. So there they are. All the guys are coming up to them because they are "the brothers." So they stand around listening to the three and ask them more questions. While everyone is resting, these three guys are out there throwing rocks, splitting hairs at 100 yards. They do it right-handed and left-handed. They are constantly moving, shaking.

Shammah's got it going, telling stories loudly all the time, and Eleazar is sweating and nervous. Notice something about the three men who are closest to David. All of them are active and eager. They are not couch potatoes. In their blood, in their lineage, all of them are eager to be doing something. Loud, nervous, singing…they're wired! David wants guys like these there. He doesn't want bored, dry company. He wants somebody to get close to him who can tell him, "We can do this! Give me my mountain! We're going to win. We can keep this bean field! David, you're going to be the man. Success to David!"

Now here comes David from the back of the cave, and he hears them talking, and he asks, "What's happening?" They say, "The Philistines have built a garrison around Bethlehem, and we can't get into the city." And David just walked away and sighed, "Oh, man, for a drink of water at the gate of Bethlehem…"

These mighty men just looked at each other as David walked away, and they winked, as if saying to each other, "Let's go do this for him." They waited until David got to the back of the cave, and they took off, not telling anyone about their plan. All the others stood around wondering where they went.

When these three got to Bethlehem, they met the Philistine garrison. Now, these guys are not some super-slick, super-intelligent, suave beings that can manipulate and talk their way into getting the water. When they walked up to the Philistine garrison, one of them was singing, one of them was sweating, and one of them was talking very loud.

Shammah said, "We came to get some water!" Eleazar, moving closer, says, "Yeah. Where is it?" And good-looking Adino was singing, "We're going to get some water. Yes, we came to get some water…" The Philistines had to be thinking, *What is up with these hyper, nervous boys?*

They got closer and closer. The Philistines asked, "What do you guys want?" The mighty men responded, "Our friend, David, told us he wanted some water, and we are here to take it." The Philistines replied, "There's 4,500 of us here, and there's three of you. How do you think you are going to get this water?"

One of the mighty men asked, "Have you ever heard of David?" A Philistine soldier responded, "You mean David, who killed Goliath, who belonged to us at one time?" The mighty men proudly declared, "Yeah, that David. He's thirsty. He wants some water." A chorus of Philistines joined together in saying, "Well, you had better find yourselves another place." But these three courageous characters refused to buy into the odds against them and responded, "No, 'cause when we heard him talk about water, he mentioned this place called the gate. Isn't that the gate of Bethlehem over there behind you? We plan to get water from there."

A tall Philistine stepped out from behind the garrison saying, "You three fools need to turn around and go back to your hole in the ground." So Shammah said, in his loud voice, "Did you hear what he said?" Eleazar said, "I love this. I was hoping you'd say something like that. I've been looking for an opportunity to take you out! Yeah, I love to fight."

The Philistines must have been puzzled, while Adino was singing, "We're going to get some water." A Philistine asked, "What's up with the pretty boy in the middle?" Adino responded, "Oh, I hate being called that. Like my brother said, we came to get some water. Now, either you're going to move, or we're going to take you out."

So the Philistines responded with derision, "Sure, take us out."

Now, watch what three mighty men will do when their leader needs something. The Bible says that they fought their way through the enemy, filled up the water flask, turned around, and fought their way back. Can't you just see this? Adino is using his spear, Eleazar still has that sword, and Shammah is fighting as well. They break through, get the water, turn around, and say, "All right! It's you again! We couldn't wait to whip you again! Please step up here."

After this victory, they returned to the cave—sweating, dirty, with Philistine blood on them, maybe a few scratches on their faces and arms. Here came the people out of the cave asking, "Where have you been?" The three responded, saying, "We went to get some water."

"Where did you get water?" asked the men.

"Where David said to go," The three answered.

David made his way through the crowd of warriors and faced his three friends. They offered the water to him, and he started crying. He broke down, saying, "I didn't mean that I wanted you to risk your lives for just a cup of water. I just wanted to taste the water of Bethlehem. I had no idea..."

He took the water, and said, "This is the blood of the men that love me. I can't drink this." Can you imagine the emotion that ran through that cave? Can you imagine the tears of those 400 men in that cave, crying as three men stood valiantly before them? These tired men—one with a sword, one with a spear, and one with a tremendous voice—said, "We just did what you said." They were willing to risk their lives just to get David a drink from his favorite drinking hole!

Wouldn't it be powerful if God's people would come together, without being cajoled and dragged? What if we caught this passion for our King? What if just a word from the Master's lips would cause us to rise and sacrifice our lives for the will of the King? It is so critical that we see the restoration of a new company of men and women who have only one concern—the will of their Lord. God wants you to be one of His mighty men and women.

Later on, Jesus had His three men who were close to Him, and all three of them were fighters. James and John were referred to as the "sons of thunder." And the third one was Simon Peter—the impetuous one. There aren't any wimps in the kingdom of God. If you are a wimp, you won't last. The toughest men and women in the world belong to the body of Christ. It's a spiritual thing. Their power is in the fact that they are not interested in themselves, and they have discovered a new source of power in the one they serve. They are interested in establishing the kingdom of God, and are willing to die for that cause.

It will take great courage for us to let go of all the treacherous and tempting things of this world and choose to embrace the cause of Christ. It will take great courage to say no to ourselves and yes to God. It might cost us a great deal, but in the end the joy of victory will overcome the agony of defeat.

CHARACTER SKETCH—COURAGE
Abraham Lincoln

ABRAHAM LINCOLN WAS BORN IN 1809 and died in 1865. The story of Abraham Lincoln is a story of courage and commitment. His nicknames give insight into how others would characterize him—Honest Abe and the Great Emancipator. Lincoln was known for his personal integrity and his unwillingness to sacrifice the truth for his personal agendas. Unlike many in the political world today, Lincoln would not build his career on perjury or propaganda in order to advance his policies or further his career. Flowing out of his commitment to integrity was his personal courage in the face of failure and tragedy. In fact, these two character qualities are twins in that it takes courage to walk in integrity and it is because of integrity that one is willing to face all opposition in order to stand for truth. In a time when the nation was facing its greatest test, it was Lincoln's courage that guided America through those tempestuous times.

Lincoln's belief in the equality of all men guided him throughout his life, and was reflected as one of the introductory statements in his legendary message given at Gettysburg during the Civil War. The conviction that all men are created equal would lead him to take a courageous stand against slavery when very powerful people stood against him. It was not a popular stand and his conviction would lead the country to the brink of destruction. But his courage and leadership would also help the country to survive those testing times.

Lincoln's pathway to the White House was not an easy road. It was fraught with failure and laden with disappointment. When he was eight years old, he suffered the death of his mother. Later he would fail at many jobs (storekeeper, postmaster), watch as one of his small businesses failed, and endure the death of three of his children. In 1855 Lincoln ran for the Senate and was defeated. The following year he ran for vice president and was defeated once again. But over and over again Lincoln found the courage to keep coming back even in the face of such personal pain and political failure.

At the age of twenty-three, he was elected to the Illinois General Assembly, a defining point in his life. But after that he went through several years of disappointment and failure. After the loss of several business ventures, he got a hold of William Blackstone's Commentary on the Laws of England. Lincoln became a self-taught lawyer, and in 1837 he was admitted into the Illinois Bar. It would be his legal practice that would set the foundation for his future work. Lincoln quickly gained the respect of his peers as an Illinois lawyer. Lincoln had finally found his calling, and as a lawyer he was very successful.

With Lincoln, failure was never final, and his perseverance, hard work, and belief in himself and his convictions eventually led him to the White House. In 1860 Lincoln became the sixteenth president of the United States of America.

One of the defining tests of leadership is one's ability to adhere to character values, such as truth even when money and power make it unpopular. The first couple of years as president, Lincoln was pulled in different directions by polarized political groups, each pleading their case for why they were right. Looming on the horizon was a serious conflict over states' rights and the issue of war. Even his own party asked him to resign. His re-election would secure his power and give him the strength to stand for his convictions on the equality of all men. He would face the fury of the southern states that insisted on their right to maintain their positions on slavery. In order to maintain peace within the Union, it would have been easier for Lincoln to simply compromise. But to choose that path would be contrary to everything he believed in. His courage to stand for his convictions would mean that he would have to run the risk of a divided nation. Lincoln put his face to the wind of controversy and would not be denied the dream that he had for America and for every soul that lived within its borders.

In 1861 the South seceded from the Union, launching the beginning of the Civil War. The war would not end until April of 1865 when Lee surrendered to Grant. Brother fought against brother, and sons were often separated from their fathers by the color of uniform they were convicted to wear. Every day Lincoln faced the death of a rising nation because of the blood that was shed by the sons that it had birthed. Each man laid down his life for what he believed was right, true, and best for the future of his children. Honest Abe maintained his integrity throughout his tenure as president, and had the courage to stand tall for freedom and equality, all the while knowing that it could very well cost him his life. From Abraham Lincoln's own lips came these words, "I do not consider that I have ever accomplished anything without God: and if it is His will that I must die by the hand of an assassin, I must be resigned. I must do my duty as I see it, and leave the rest to God."

On April 14, 1865, while Lincoln was watching a theatrical performance at Ford's Theater in Washington, D.C., John Wilkes Booth, an actor who was angry with Lincoln because of the defeat of the Confederacy, shot him.

Lincoln's courage in the face of such enormous opposition and the possibility of the dissolution of the Union that he loved did not deter him from doing what was right. He had the courage to stand tall at a time when this country needed such a man to reverse the curse of slavery. Lincoln would not be able to see the fulfillment of his dream but his courage would open the door for others who had a similar dream. Abraham Lincoln courageously stood for the fact that all men are created equal and should never be denied the rights that are due all men as members of the human race.

> *Let us have faith that right makes might, and in that faith, let us, to the end, dare to do our duty as we understand it.*
> —From Lincoln's Cooper Institute
> Address, February 27, 1860

Enthusiasm is one of the most powerful engines of success. When you do a thing, do it with all your might. Put your whole soul into it. Stamp it with your own personality. Be active, be energetic and faithful, and you will accomplish your object. Nothing great was ever achieved without enthusiasm.

—Ralph Waldo Emerson

CHAPTER SIX

FOLLOWING THE KING—PASSIONATE PURPOSE

HAT INNER FORCE LIFTS A man out of the mainstream of mediocrity into the lonely chase of his dream? What mysterious power is so mesmerizing that it leads one to relinquish the luxuries of life in order to respond to the lure of the unthinkable? What intriguing pursuit has the power to pull one into a circle of commitment that eliminates all other fascinations outside that ring? What sacred cause awakens a man from the slumber of indifference to pursue the scent of the impossible?

This strange phenomenon is called passion. Passion is the fire of life and the energy of the soul! It is the wind that gives loft to the eagle, lifting it above the masses locked in the drudgery of apathetic inactivity. It is the fire that warms the heart in the midst of the coldness of a culture set adrift. It is a man's friend in the dark hours of the night when others abandon him. It is the inner support that keeps him awake in the night seasons when others are fast asleep. It is the power for the race, the propulsion for the jet, the spark for the fire, the wind for the sail, and the contractions for the birth.

Every successful man and woman has experienced the transforming power of passion. Like a silent hunter, this unseen force captured them with its reality and catapulted them into the race for the inaccessible. These men and women became its prisoners, coerced by the allurement of its dreams.

This kind of success demands that a man reach deep down within himself for an inner strength that can be produced only by this passionate zeal.

Passion brings forth a harvest of dreamers and visionaries. It is the dynamic link that connects a dream to its reality. A dream is not enough; it always must be accompanied by the intensity of passion that drives one into the lonely arena reserved for those who attempt the impossible and track the invisible.

Those who have not seen the invisible realities of their dream worlds think such people are mad. The contented are disturbed by their zeal and fervor. The elite misinterpret the driven actions of such people as a direct assault on them. All isolate them for fear of catching this horrible disease that challenges one to move outside the comfort of the traditional and conventional. They endeavor to segregate these people in order to safeguard their own comfortable and secure lifestyles.

Not every passion is legitimate. Some passions are destructive and even dangerous. The drive for wealth, fame, and power can motivate people to betrayal and domination of others. It can possess them to the point where they manipulate those around them and destroy their own souls.

In spite of the fact that some passions can be negative, you must understand that you cannot achieve anything without passion. Without the fire of passion, a person will slip back into the slough of mediocrity and be tempted to return to the shelter of anonymity. The absence of passion will leave one isolated in his own fantasy world, always dreaming of the great possibilities of life but never committing himself to their fulfillment. If you discover the passion behind a man's success, you will have found the key that unlocks the door to his dream world.[1]

PASSIONS ARE POWERFUL

David was a passionate man. He did *everything* with great passion. As we examine his life, we see that when he focused and channeled his passions toward God's purpose, he was very successful. On the other hand, when his passions went uncontrolled, such as his encounter with Bathsheba, it brought tremendous devastation to his life. Uncontrolled passions can be detrimental. When a man undergoes transformation in his life, and he moves from darkness toward the light, he discovers a profound ability to focus his passion on God, resulting in fulfillment and success.

In Proverbs 25:28, Solomon, son of David, wrote that a man without self-control is like a city without walls. A man who does not know how to control or direct his passion will be overcome by all sorts of evil. In contrast, the man who has discovered how to control and focus his passion will be able to do anything.

Other words that describe passion include: vehemence, desire, enthusiasm, delight, rage, fire, fervor, zeal, and heat. Let's talk about setting your passion. You have the ability to set your passion. If you can't control your passion—your desire—it can kill you. Passion is contagious. John Wesley said that if a man sets himself on fire, people would come watch him burn. If I have five minutes with a person, they will feel the fire that is burning in my soul. They will see the vision that has driven my life. As you listen, some portion of that passionate vision will grab hold of you because passion is contagious.

Michael Jordan could be talking to you about his passion for basketball, and you may not get any kind of desire to play basketball, but you may get a desire to be productive or successful in whatever you're doing, by mere fact of his zeal. That's why athletes often make great motivational speakers, because they know about the power of passion.

There is a potion in passion that will affect the people around you. In Psalm 42:1, the psalmist says, *As the deer pants for streams of water, so my soul pants for you, O God.* Now, that is very descriptive. Verse 2 says, *My soul thirsts for God, for the living God.* Does that sound like a man desperate and committed to experiencing God? And it continues, *When can I go and meet with God?* This is a man who is driven.

Have you ever seen a deer that is panting? For a deer to pant, he has to be running for his life. He's running for his life with his mind locked on one thing—water, cool refreshing water. Like the deer charging down through forest trails in search of the streams, making their way through the wooded terrain, so David searched with all of his heart for the living God.

It is sad when we lose our passion and fire, and it does happen. Why did we change, from the time we were filled with the Holy Ghost—a time when we were on our knees praying, seeking God, fasting, reading the Word, pushing the plate back, witnessing everywhere we went, telling people about Jesus? But now we're "mature." The writer says ...*as the hart panteth after the water brooks, so panteth my soul after thee, O God* (v. 1, KJV). Then he breaks it down and says, "When am I going to meet you?"

I have a strong conviction about Keith Green. I am not one to build monuments to men, but Keith Green had a tremendous passion to see Jesus Christ. He was a prophet to my generation. He stood flat-footed and talked to musicians about not charging admission fees for concerts. He challenged the accepted protocol of the church. He stood before us in his blue jeans and T-shirts, and long hair, and challenged even the theologians about their teachings and lifestyle.

I asked God why He had taken him away. One day my wife and I were having this discussion because he and his wife were a very powerful influence in our lives. My wife, Robin, said, "I believe that his passion for God was so strong—you could hear it in his songs. 'I only want to see You…I want to see You… When can I see You?…' His passion to see God was so strong that God could not resist his passion to see Him any more."

HAPPINESS IS LIVING WITH PASSION

That is deep, but I believe it. All he talked about was his desire to see Jesus. Matthew 5:6 powerfully declares, *"Blessed are those who hunger and thirst for righteousness, for they will be filled." Happiness is living with passion.* If you consider what Jesus' words meant, He is drawing a verbal picture of a man who is hungry and thirsty—ravenously crazy for a crumb of bread and dying for just one drink of water. Jesus said that people with this kind of intense passion are blessed, happy, and they will be filled.

The story is told of a preacher baptizing a young man in a river, and as he said, "I baptize you in the name of Jesus," he took him under the water and held him under. The boy started squirming, and the preacher held him. The boy started kicking water above the surface, splashing everywhere, and the preacher held him under. The boy was getting upset by then, and he was wiggling, trying to get away, and still the preacher held him under. Finally the boy slipped out of the preacher's hands, hit the preacher and knocked him back, and came out gasping for air. The preacher looked at him and said, "What did you want more than anything when I was holding you under that water?" The boy said, "Air." He said, "When you want God as much as you wanted air, you shall be filled."

God should never be taken as an add-on to the other things in our lives. He will not allow that. Paul said in Colossians 3:1-4, *Since, then, you have been raised with Christ, set your hearts on things above, where Christ is seated at the right hand of God. Set your minds on things above, not on earthly things. For you died, and your life is now hidden with Christ in God. When Christ, who is your life, appears, then you also will appear with him in glory.*

The King James Version instructs us in verse one to ...*seek those things which are above....* The word *seek* means "to desire for, or to be passionate after." Be passionate. Desire things that are above. Verse two says, *Set your minds.*

To set your mind means "to exercise the mind." It also means to interest oneself in something with concern, or obedience. When do you become interested in something? Can you just say, "Okay, I'm interested in this?" It doesn't happen. I just quizzed Robin today, asking her what it would take for her to be interested in sports. She said, "It won't happen. I'm not interested." I asked, "How, then, can you make yourself do this?" She looked at me with a puzzled expression. I said, "Let me explain something to you. There is one thing that we don't have a choice about. When you talk about eternity, you don't have a decision."

When you are seated with Christ in the heavenly realms, you don't have to decide whether or not you're interested in the things of God. I might want to read my Bible. I might want to pray. I might want to go to church. It's not a decision.

CHOICES LEAD TO PASSION

In Christ there is no such thing as indecision. You've already made your choice. Therefore, Paul says to set, seek, fix, arrange, and exercise your mind by discipline and obedience. The result of this is that the more you exercise dominion of your mind in reading the Word of God, thinking about the things of God, and doing the work of the ministry, the more interested you become in it. Focus and exposure create passion! In other words, if I expose you to something long enough, you will be affected. And this is what he's talking about.

Paul is warning us, pointing out how easy it is to let your passions run away from you if you don't train yourself through obedience and discipline to read, to study, to pray, to attend church, to worship, and to praise when you don't feel like it. No prayer, no power. No praise, no power.

Now, without set passions, it is impossible to discover purpose. We must establish our purpose. Romans 12:1 says, *Therefore, I urge you, brothers, in view of God's mercy, to offer your bodies as living sacrifices, holy and pleasing to God—this is your spiritual act of worship.* He's writing this to Christians. He is concerned that the world's systems have been negatively influencing these believers. The world had its own accepted rules of behavior and order of morality. But Paul told the Romans, *Do not conform any longer to the pattern of this world, but be transformed by the renewing of your mind* (v. 2).

What does the word *set* mean in Colossians 3:2? It means to exercise your mind. This is powerful. After you do this, *then you will be able to test and approve what God's will is—his good, pleasing and perfect will* (Romans 12:2), which is His purpose for your life. People don't know why they're here. You may be convinced that you are here just to go to your 9-to-5 job and get enough money to eat a meal today. That is your life. You exist to get to Saturday, and you might go to church on Sunday.

But the truth is that you were created for a specific task. God made you…He put affections in you…He put passions in you…He put desires in you…He put holy ambition in you, for you to be and to do what He created you to be and do. Let me qualify that. This doesn't mean that you need to quit your job and trust God that your money will come in through the mailbox. We are created as God's workmanship to do good works in Christ. Those good works can be through your job. You can express God's purpose through your occupation.

In fact, it is God's desire that you passionately extend His kingdom into the marketplace. Where you work and what you do is more than a mere job. It is a means for expressing God's purpose through your life. Until you get a vision of His purposes for your life then you will never be able to tap into that divine passion reserved for you.

ENSLAVED TO YOUR ASSIGNMENT

What is your goal? Where will you be ten years from now? Have you thought about that? Or are you thinking that you're going to be doing the same thing you're doing now? You have to have a passion for your purpose. Paul says: "I beseech you, in view of God's mercy, to offer yourselves as a living sacrifice…" Die to yourself, so that you can find what that perfect pleasing will of God is. That's your purpose. Paul was a driven man. He was very passionate about what he did. He saw a man in a vision in Macedonia, telling him to come and visit, and he went.

Paul realized that the vision was from God. He saw it as clearly as if the man were standing right in front of him. Everywhere he went, he told everybody what happened on the way to Damascus. He told them the whole story. So here he was in Antioch, bringing up the Old Testament, the prophet Samuel, and telling these people, *"Then the people asked for a king, and he gave them Saul son of Kish, of the tribe of Benjamin, who ruled forty years. After removing Saul, he made David their king. He testified concerning him: 'I have found David son of Jesse a man after my own heart; he will do everything I want him to do'"* (Acts 13:21, 22).

David's heart, his seat of passion, in spite of all of his mistakes, was a heart that declared that he loved God more than Bathsheba, Amnon, Absalom, Tamar, Abishag, and Abigail. His heart and his passion decreed that he loved God more than his houses and his palaces, his horses and his mule.

David loved God more than he loved anything. This is why God could say that He had found a man whose heart was toward Him. Second Chronicles 16:9 says that *…the eyes of the Lord range throughout the earth to strengthen those whose hearts are fully committed to him….* God is searching for a man to show himself strong. He is looking for somebody. Who's looking for Him? While God is looking for you, you ought to be passionately looking for God.

In Acts 13:36, Paul continues talking about David, saying that *"…when David had served God's purpose in his own genera-*

tion, he fell asleep; he was buried with his fathers and his body decayed." The word *served* in this context means "to be subordinate, under the order." What did David do with passion? He served his purpose. He was subordinate—under the control of his purpose. Passion was submitted to divine purpose! Nothing was allowed in his life that violated his purpose. His passion was for his purpose. This is powerful. The key to David's success is that he served his purpose. *He was enslaved by his assignment.*

Yes, David failed because of his passions, but I'm going to show you what happens when passion kisses purpose. When David was about twelve years old, Samuel came to the house of Jesse, David's father, found the boy, recognized him for who he was, and anointed him with oil. Now, there was a war going on between the Israelites and the Philistines during this time. A few days after the anointing ceremony, Jesse sent young David to take some cheese and bread to his brothers on the front lines of war. This teenager obediently took cheese and bread and left his father's house.

PASSION EMBRACES PURPOSE

But guess what he has? He has more than cheese and bread. He has oil on his head. That's his purpose, his assignment. The anointing of oil meant that he would be Israel's king. He was sent to serve his brothers on this trip, but the day would come when his brothers would serve him. Right now he is an adolescent with raging hormones. All he knows is that Samuel said he was going to be king, and David trusted the prophet.

He arrived at the battlefield, and heard someone screaming with a voice like thunder. Guess what he was screaming about? He was screaming about David's domain—Goliath the Philistine giant was defying the kid's domain. David knew this was his territory. Samuel had told him it was, and not only that, the Word said it was.

First Samuel 17:26 says, *David asked the men standing near him, "What will be done for the man who kills this Philistine and removes this disgrace from Israel? Who is this uncircumcised Philistine that he should defy the armies of the living God?"* The Bible goes on to say in verses 28-30 that David looked over at his handsome older brother, Eliab, and asked, "What are you doing about that man defying the armies of the living God? He's defying my country." We all know what lots of older brothers think about their mouthy, younger siblings. Can't you just imagine Eliab saying, "Shut up, David, you conceited, prideful pup. You're just out here to see how a battle is fought and to show off. Why don't you just go on home to Daddy?" But David asks, *"Can't I even speak?" He then turned away to someone else and brought up the same matter, and the men answered him as before* (vv. 29,30).

What was really happening here? May I submit to you that *passion was beginning to embrace purpose?* A powerful force was arising on the inside of this kid. He had had some experience with these feelings before. He had faced down and killed both a lion and a bear that were attacking his territory, and David knew he had something within him that responded forcefully when someone or something threatened his domain.

There stood Goliath. The Bible says, *For forty days the Philistine came forward every morning and evening and took his stand* (1 Samuel 17:16). Morning and night he had challenged the armies of Saul to send out a man who could fight and kill him.

In your mind's eye, see this kid stand up and say, "I'm here."

Goliath was insulted. If you read all of 1 Samuel 17, you'll find that Goliath looked at David and despised him. *He said to*

David, "Am I a dog, that you come at me with sticks?" And the Philistine cursed David by his gods. "Come here," he said, "and I'll give your flesh to the birds of the air and the beasts of the field!" (vv. 43,44).

And David's passion is ignited—his vehemence, his fire, is lit and is swirling around inside him. What is happening? Passion is embracing purpose, and something is happening in this kid's life to the point that he can't stand it any more. In David's mind, he knows that he was born to extinguish Goliath. What is happening? His passion is meeting his purpose. He took his shepherd bag and went out to meet the giant. He looked at him and said, *"This day the Lord will hand you over to me, and I'll strike you down and cut off your head. Today I will give the carcasses of the Philistine army to the birds of the air and the beasts of the earth, and the whole world will know that there is a God in Israel" (v. 46).*

The Bible says that the Israelite army was quaking with fear. But here's a kid, looking at this giant saying, "Something's burning in me. I'm sick of you."

When you get set...when you get fixed...when you get your affections focused, you are a powerful person. This boy met his destiny. He woke up with cheese and bread, and by the time the dew hit the ground, David was kissing his destiny. He was not worried about Goliath. When you allow your passions and affections to be set, you are able to approve what God's will is for your life. You will look at whatever is facing you and defend your territory. You will tell the enemy to move. You'll just do what you do best.

David was an incredible warrior. That boy was a "bad fighter." He killed the champion. The Bible refers to Goliath as the champion of the Philistines—the "baddest" of the bad. But when Goliath came up against passion and purpose, he was no match. If you're not going to serve with all your heart, just stay at the house. If you're not going to minister where your passion kisses your purpose, don't minister. If you can't porter with passion, it's better that you don't do it at all. We need to be overtaken.

PASSION FOR EXCELLENCE IN YOUR PURPOSE GUARANTEES PROSPERITY

When you can represent vision with excellence, it moves people. When you can tell a man your vision with tears in your eyes, all of a sudden passion takes over and you'll compel people to support your vision. The passion of Jesus kissed the purpose of Jesus and changed the hearts of all those who came in contact with Him. Jesus Christ went about doing good, healing all that were oppressed by the devil. He was on a mission. He set His face like flint to go to Jerusalem. When He walked through Samaria, He knew exactly where He was going.

Where are you going? What are you passionate about? Are you passionate about waking up in the morning? What drives you? Let's go deeper. If your goal in life is to pray, that is not a goal. That is an opportunity. It is a foregone conclusion. You are supposed to talk to God! What is your goal? What is your purpose? Why are you here? When you find out, be passionate about it. Passion is doing what you love and loving what you do. Don't be miserable—do what you love and love what you do. Find your purpose and get passionate about it.

We have already mentioned how uncontrolled passions can be very detrimental, but now I want to emphasize how focused passions can be very beneficial and make you very successful. But you must learn how to give your passions to God in such a way that they will be consecrated and sanctified to Him in the Spirit.

David was a real man who was emotionally up one day and down the next. He experienced every extremity of emotions and experiences that life had to offer. The underlying current in his life was the fact that God said, speaking to Saul through the prophet Samuel, "I have found a man who is after my heart."

David would establish for future generations what it meant to know and walk with God. In 2 Samuel 23, we find him in the waning years of his life. His life was nearly over. He wrote his song of praise in this chapter and listed his thirty-seven mighty men. I find it very interesting that the thirty-seventh one, or the last one mentioned in verse 39, is Uriah the Hittite, who was Bathsheba's husband. It is interesting that in this list of the mighty men of David, we find the very one who would be his point of failure.

Because of his passion for Bathsheba, David had Uriah the Hittite killed by putting him in the front lines of battle, knowing that he would be the first to die. I've mentioned all of that to say that David had served God in three different areas in his life. **He was a shepherd**—a good shepherd. **He was a warrior**—a good warrior. **And he was a king**—a good king.

It is interesting that David never surrounded himself with shepherds. He never surrounded himself with kings. But he did surround himself with warriors, because more than anything else, he was a man of war. In fact, God said, *You are not to build a house for my Name, because you are a warrior and have shed blood* (1 Chronicles 28:3).

Even though David had a great desire to see the house of God built, it was his son, Solomon, who would build it, and David encouraged him to be courageous in getting it done.

The vision for the temple was birthed in the heart of David, as recorded in 1 Chronicles 28, but he would not live to see the temple completed, for David was a warrior. The ingredient that I want to expose to you more than any other thing in the life of David is that he was first and foremost a fighter. He knew how to fight.

We live in a society that is draped in the cloak of nothingness. I have seen young people wearing T-shirts with the words, "Now I'm Nothing" printed on the back of them, like that is the whole pursuit: to be nothing; just to blend in. Thus, it's even displayed in dress—don't cause any disruption, don't disturb anything, just fit in, just go along. This existential philosophy has robbed our generation of the vitality and vision necessary to become all they were destined to be.

It's almost like the '60s mentality is coming back: chill out, get some big flowers on your jeans, and just blend in. "Tune in, turn on, and drop out." What a philosophy of life! Christianity has never been the call to do and be nothing. If the zeal of God consumes you like it did our forefathers, there will always be the drive to do more. The dark void of nothingness must not be allowed in the ranks of the army of God. The example of Christ as He lived His life with the words, "I must" chained to His heart has to be the anthem of every saint of God.

DRIVEN BY PURPOSE

Jesus was a man driven by passion for His purpose. At the synagogue, when He was twelve years old, we find Him saying to His mother, "*I must* be about my Father's business" (see Luke 2:49). At the well, with the woman who had been married five times, we find Him telling His disciples, "I *must* finish the work" (see John 4). In John 9:4, replying to the disciples' questions after healing a man born blind, He said, *"As long as it is day, we must do the work of him who sent me. Night is coming, when no one can work."* He was a driven man—He was driven with passion.

Why should we, His followers, be any less driven? The apathetic attitude that has invaded the church of Christ must be exposed and expelled. I don't know about you, but I want to die tired and satisfied, knowing that I have given my all for the purposes of God.

David's mighty men joined with him as warriors, with purpose. As we have seen, one of the greatest of those mighty men was Eleazar, who was a man full of passion. Passion for purpose is contagious, and Eleazar was a contagious man.

> *Next to him was Eleazar the son of Dodai the Ahohite. As one of the three mighty men, he was with David when they taunted the Philistines gathered at Pas Dammim for battle. Then the men of Israel retreated, but he stood his ground and struck down the Philistines till his hand grew tired and froze to the sword. The Lord brought about a great victory that day. The troops returned to Eleazar, but only to strip the dead.*
>
> —2 Samuel 23:9,10

Eleazar manifested great passion in all that he did. He was not afraid of the Philistines. His courage was contagious. The word *contagious* means "to spread by contact." Men of passion are attractive and contagious.

Jesus was a man driven by purpose, which was the cross. He was so driven by His passion that He could walk up to fishermen and tax collectors, look at them, and say, "Follow

Me," and the influence was so great as manifested on His face, through His voice, in His heart, and the whole demeanor of His life, that people literally put down their nets, quit their jobs, walked away from anything that was holding them back, and followed Him. Why? Simply because He knew what He was doing, where He was going, and wasn't about doing nothing— He was *always* about doing something.

Thus, David was a very dangerous man to the enemies of Israel. He was a man with passion for his purpose, and he attracted men with great courage and passion. Men with passion and purpose are dangerous to the established order. Even when that man is driven into a cave, you had better be careful because he is a man of passionate purpose, and he will draw other warriors to him. Four hundred men eventually found him, because they wanted to hang around somebody who knew what he was doing, what his purpose was, and where he was going.

It takes a leader to know a leader, to grow a leader, and to show a leader. Eleazar was a great warrior because he hung out and lived with a great warrior. I always say, if you tell me who you hang around with, I'll tell you who you are. Eleazar knew more than shepherding…more than kingship. He learned to fight because he stayed with David when he was down, and when he was up. He was *with* David.

David lived his life with men who were just like him surrounding him—men who were going to succeed him and perpetuate his kingdom. He knew that neither shepherding nor kingship was going to advance the kingdom of Israel. He knew it was going to take men of tenacity, men of war, fighting men who were not double-minded, but who knew who they were, who knew their purpose, and had a passion to complete it.

Always stay in the company of people who know what they're doing and know where they're going. If you start hanging around with wanderers, you will begin to wander. Of all the people in the world, Christians ought to know what we're doing, what we're about, what our agenda is, what our objectives are, what our goals are, personally, individually, and as a church. This world needs to look at you and know who you are just as the people in Samaria looked at Jesus and noticed that He was special. He was unique. He wasn't exactly like them.

He had a look about Him—there was something about His countenance that said, "I know who I am and where I am going," and many followed Him. If people can look at you and not recognize you as a child of God, something's wrong. If you don't know what you're doing or where you're going, you won't influence anyone.

In 1 Samuel 14:1-14, we find a story of two young men. Jonathan is a natural born leader—a man with passion and purpose. He knew how to submit his position to one who was greater. He was a man who was not about doing nothing, but about doing something, and whose father was backslidden eighteen miles in the wrong direction (when he should have been in Geba, he was in Bibeah. He was in the wrong place).

So here was Jonathan, a bored-stiff teenager, who said to his armor-bearer, "*Come, let's go over to the outpost of those uncircumcised fellows. Perhaps the Lord will act in our behalf. Nothing can hinder the Lord from saving, whether by many or by few*" (v. 6). In other words, "I don't know about you, but I'm not going to sit around here all day. My father is in the wrong place, the armies of Israel are hiding in the thickets, caves, and holes in the ground, and I'm about to do something."

The young armor-bearer catches the *disease* of passion and looks at Jonathan. *"Do all that you have in mind,"* his armor-bearer said. *"Go ahead; I am with you heart and soul"* (v. 7). He had caught the passion and vision as if it were the flu! And what happened? Verses 13 and 14 say, *Jonathan climbed up, using his hands and feet, with his armor-bearer right behind him. The Philistines fell before Jonathan, and his armor-bearer followed and killed behind him. In that first attack, Jonathan and his armor-bearer killed some twenty men in an area of about half an acre.* Be sure about who you have standing next to you.

Eleazar was with David the same way the armor-bearer was with Jonathan. If David was in Adullam, Eleazar was in Adullam. If David was in the palace, Eleazar was in the palace. He was listed, not just as one of the mighty men, but as one of the top three. The Bible says that they were all mighty men. I want you to notice his passionate loyalty to David. *He was with David.*

ATTEMPT BIG THINGS, ATTRACT BIG MEN

A French official addressing Winston Churchill once said, "If you are doing big things, you will attract big men. If you are doing little things, you attract little men, and it's the little men that cause trouble." What I eat, drink, and sleep is the vision of my church. There is no doubt that it will come to pass. But, I tell you, the moment that vision becomes small enough for me to do it, I've just eliminated God from the whole process. If I can accomplish it, it's not God.

If we can keep this vision big enough that men in every class of society will look at us and say, "Wow, I like that!" they will bow in reverence to the fact that you are driven with passion for your purpose. But this is just one, small, intricate detail of

Christianity. I just happen to be a preacher. But what are you? Who are you? How are you? And where are you?

When you have a passion for purpose, people are attracted to you. David had no problem drawing a crowd, just because he knew who he was, and he knew where he was going. Passion for purpose takes courage.

There is a story about Abraham Lincoln standing at the Port of New Orleans. A ship docked at the port and slaves started coming off that ship. Abraham Lincoln watched with his hands grasping his waist. He saw a family disembark the ship—a father, mother, and a young boy. Just as they stepped off the ship, they were sold immediately to three different slave owners. It deeply stirred the heart of Abraham Lincoln...to the point that his fingernails pierced his palms, and blood dripped from the ends of his fingers onto the dock. He looked at his companion with tears in his eyes, and said these words: "One day, I'm going to be the president of the United States of America, and I'm going to abolish slavery."

He knew why he was born. There was not a doubt in his mind. So Abraham Lincoln ran for president and lost. He ran again and lost. He ran again and again—running for public office and losing ten times. After the tenth time, he suffered a nervous breakdown and was committed to a mental institution for a year. When he recovered, he came out saying, "I'm going to be the president of the United States of America." He ran the eleventh time, and he was elected president of the United States of America, and the first thing he did was abolish slavery. Why? Because he had the courage to stand alone and the passion to overcome his failure on the way to his purpose.

Many times our problem is that we're not sure of our purpose and, therefore, instead of being encouraged, we get discouraged, lose heart, give up, and say, "I missed God." Perhaps you have prayed for something, and when it looked like God had spoken, you declared, "God said it." But when it didn't work out the way you wanted it to, then you said, "I must have been wrong," and you lost courage. The definition of *courage* is "the ability to face defeat and difficulty with firmness and no fear."

ONE MAN WITH PASSION IS A MAJORITY

Eleazar was a man of courage. When all of Israel had retreated, he said, "Bring it on. I was born to kill all of you." How can a man stand and kill men like that? Because God said it, and based upon His Word, it can be done. It doesn't matter what anyone else is doing.

When you are driven with passion for your purpose, you're a bold man or woman. You are courageous and determined. Let me tell you a secret: It doesn't just take intelligence to do great things—it takes courage too.

Determined teams win championships, not great teams. You can't take the same caliber of athletes and pay them all that money and not have a winner. What separates the great from the average is courage and determination. Give me a group of people—it doesn't matter where they are—who will come together and say, "Come hell or high water, we're going to do this thing in Jesus' name," and we can do anything we so desire.

Paul's last letter to his son Timothy was the last letter he would ever write. Timothy is his spiritual son with whom he was very careful with his words. In 2 Timothy 4:14,15, he says, *Alexander the metalworker did me a great deal of harm. The Lord will repay him for what he has done. You too should be on your guard against him, because he strongly opposed our message.* In my own words, I translate that verse like this, "Look, Tim,

Alexander the metal worker has done it again. He has really done some harm this time. But that's all right, son, because God is going to pay him back."

Paul was in prison when he wrote this letter to his son, and he said in verses 16 and 17, *At my first defense, no one came to my support, but everyone deserted me. May it not be held against them. But the Lord stood at my side and gave me strength, so that through me the message might be fully proclaimed and all the Gentiles might hear it…*. Take a man that has passion for purpose, and he is driven by that purpose. What we see will create passion. Put that passionate man in a prison, and he'll write two thirds of the New Testament. You can't stop a man full of passion for purpose.

You can knock him down and take the wind out of him, but somehow he'll come climbing back. He might be scratched up, dirty or beat up, but he is looking for purpose. He is in search of his objective. He will fulfill his vision. That's why Paul said, "They beat me thirty nine times and left me out in the street, but I'm back. I must preach the gospel; it's not an option for me." (See 2 Corinthians 11:24.)

WRESTLING FOR YOUR PURPOSE

In Genesis 32:24-32, we read about Jacob struggling with God all night, until he won the victory, and his name was changed to Israel. You have to get hold of a purpose that will change your life and hold onto it all night long. Don't leave the thing until you can walk differently…until you can talk differently. Verse 32 says, *to this day the Israelites do not eat the tendon attached to the socket of the hip, because the socket of Jacob's hip was touched near the tendon.* After the night of wrestling with God, Jacob walked differently. He had been looked upon as the deceiver, but after one night of wrestling with destiny, Jacob became Israel.

There have been times when I've had to wrestle for my calling. Sometimes you have to wrestle with your own mind and your own flesh and just knock it down and get ready for another one. You have to be like Eleazar. You have to be able to grab the sword and find out why you are here…why you breathe and eat…why you were born…why you were fearfully and wonderfully made.

God has a purpose for your life, and until you discover it, you will not have the passion to sustain you. Purpose will awaken the passion that is within you. It is there but it needs to find its purpose. Passionate people make a great difference. Passion for purpose completes you so that you can complete your task. A person with passion for his purpose always completes his task.

No one in the body of Christ is insignificant. I hope this agitates you to the point that you do something about your life…so that you go to work saying, "I'm going to find my assignment. God has a purpose for my life, and I must find it or I will die."

God has a special design for your life. You are a perfect fit for a unique slot in the great purposes of God in this world. When you find your purpose, then you will discover the fire of passion. It is that passion that will invigorate and sustain you until you reach the fulfillment of the divine destiny for your life.

CHARACTER SKETCH— PASSIONATE PURPOSE

Jackie Pullinger-To

JACKIE PULLINGER-TO WAS A WOMAN of purpose driven by a fiery passion because of her desire to serve disenfranchised addicts, gamblers, pornographers, gang members, and prostitutes within the walled-city of Hong Kong. In her own words she best describes the passion that drove her purpose.

"I loved the dark city. I loved wandering down the narrow lanes that were like some exaggerated stage set. It upset me to see twelve- or thirteen-year-old prostitutes and to learn that these girls were not free, having been sold by parents or boyfriends. It troubled me to meet their minders—the aged mamasans who sat on the orange boxes in the streets luring the Walled City voyeurs with promises of 'she's very good, very young, very cheap.' I noticed their hands, which were scarred on the back with needle marks from the heroin injections which made the job bearable. Or maybe the job was to pay for the heroin.

"There were bodies at that time lying in the streets near the drug dens: they could have been alive or dead after 'chasing the drag-on' (a popular way of inhaling heroin through a tube held over heated tinfoil). There were the 'weather men' who guarded the alley exits and the entrances to the heroin huts where up to a hundred people 'chased' in lonely chorus. I saw thousands of poor people living in one-room dwellings: many were so crammed that they had to sleep in shifts because they could not all lie down at the same time. I saw some who still lived with pigs, neither able to see the light of day....

"I loved this dark place. I hated what was happening in it but I wanted to be nowhere else. I dreamed of walking into heroin dens, laying hands on men and seeing them set free. I dreamed of praying with the blind in the dark lanes, touching them, and watching their eyes open. It was almost as if I could already see another city in its place and that city was ablaze with light. It was my dream. There was no more crying, no more death or pain. The sick were healed, addicts set free, the hungry filled. There were families for orphans, homes for the homeless, and new dignity for those who had lived in shame. I had no idea how to bring this about but with 'visionary zeal' imagined introducing the Walled City people to the one who could change it all: Jesus."[2]

Jackie Pullinger-To had talked about being a missionary since she was five years old, even though for many years she had no real idea what a missionary was. She had a conventional English upbringing—attending a boarding school and being confirmed in the Church of England. Higher education followed at the Royal College of Music, where Jackie studied piano and oboe. Upon completing her degree, she began a career teaching music. However, she could not escape the feeling that she needed to give her life to something greater than herself. She encountered a group of friends who obviously enjoyed their relationship with Jesus and could discuss their experience and feelings about it with ease and joy. This concept intrigued Jackie. She states, "This was the first time that I had met Christians who did not look unhappy, guilty or grim, and my music college Christian Union…had only served to confirm my worst fears and impressions of earnest organists trying to get to heaven. I preferred brass players. I avoided the Christians while unable to avoid the unhappy conviction that at some time God himself would nail me for my shortcomings, and I would have to account for my life."

After accepting Jesus as her Lord and Savior, she found herself filled with a great joy, and rather than becoming more limited and grim, her life became more fun than ever before. During this time, God reawakened within Jackie her childhood dream of becoming a missionary, but she was a single woman and too young and unqualified to be accepted by any of the conventional missionary societies. Every door seemed shut, and she wondered if she had heard God correctly. Desperate for answers and direction, Jackie attended a special prayer meeting with friends, and there God spoke to her. He said, "Go. Trust Me, and I will lead you. I will instruct you and lead you in the way in which you shall go; I will guide you with My eye."

As a true warrior, Jackie knew that she must take action and obey. After much prayer and godly counsel, Jackie decided that God had doors to open for her that she had not yet seen. She decided to allow God to lead her directly and go on a daring adventure. She bought the cheapest boat ticket she could find that stopped at the greatest number of countries, and prayed for God's direction to know where to get off and how He wanted her to proceed from there. So in 1966, with this great act of faith, Jackie found herself stepping off a boat in Hong Kong after traveling halfway around the globe. She had no missionary agency or organized support for her back in Britain, no job, and no contacts. She had very little money and no clear direction of what God had in store for her, but she had the assurance that God had called her and would continue to direct her.

Soon after her arrival in Hong Kong, Jackie was hired to teach music three afternoons a week in a primary school operated by a Mrs. Donnithorne. The school was located within a six-acre enclave of Hong Kong known as the Walled City. One of its Chinese names is "Hak Nam," which means "darkness." Cramped, secluded, and filthy, the Walled City was home to anywhere from 30,000 to 60,000 people—no one knew for sure how many—and was a haven of opium dens, heroin huts, brothels, pornography theaters, illegal gambling, smuggling, and all other kinds of vice. Virtually ignored by the rest of Hong Kong, the Walled City was accessible only through dark, narrow alleys between shops located on its outer edges. There were no sanitary facilities—refuse and excrement were simply dumped out in the streets and alleys—and electricity was illegally tapped from supplies outside the city.

Daily life in the Walled City was regulated and defined by various Triad gangs who controlled the region's activities of vice, extortion, and crime. The boundaries of each gang's territory were clearly defined, and violence between rival gangs was frequent. Gang membership provided a sense of family and acceptance for young Chinese men that they rarely found elsewhere in "Hak Nam." The city called "darkness" was in great need of the light of

Jesus, and Jackie was becoming a torchbearer for her generation. Jackie's teaching work gave her access to the Walled City, and she began trying to relate to the people she met there. She sought to share Christ as she had opportunity. Externally, the Walled City was one of the most revolting places on earth, yet every time she entered it, Jackie felt a profound sense of joy. This confirmed for her that she was where God had called her.

At first Jackie met with little success. She had zeal but few obvious results. This was made apparent one day as she tried to share Jesus with a corner prostitute: "She was an old-young prostitute who squatted all day long over a sewer with little custom and no looks. She had no radio, she could not read. She looked dead before her life had even started. I tried the 'Jesus loves you' routine on her and touched her to show her I meant it. She looked terrified. 'You've made a mistake. You don't know who I am. You're not supposed to touch people like me.'

"Looking back now, I can see how ridiculous it was to be walking down alleyways talking intensely of Jesus. Of course, no one could respond to words about Christ. They had never met Him and had no evidence of His love. When I checked, I found He had never done it that way either; instead of declaring, 'I love you,' Jesus had shown His love through action. He opened the eyes of the blind man, caused the lame to leap for joy, and fed five thousand hungry people full to bursting."[3]

This thought planted a dream deep within this radical disciple. She wanted these desperately needy people to know Jesus, but in order for them to meet Him, she realized that she must first show Him to them. Jackie began a youth club to reach out to the young people of the Walled City. This club enabled her to befriend young people who were members of the feared Triad organizations.

God touched her in a new way, and she began to pray intensely for the people within the dark Walled City. Suddenly light began to break through the darkness around her, and lives began to be changed one by one. Jackie took seriously her call to help the people at their point of need. She went to bat for the poor and helped them obtain assistance and housing from government agencies. She planned activities to give the young people alternatives to the vices around them.

She looked for ways to help and minister to the most "poor in spirit and body" of those around her, which ultimately led her to preaching Jesus and ministering to the needs of the drug addicts. Jackie discovered that a sincere heart, prayer, and praise could often help an addict go through withdrawal in a short and relatively painless way.

It was not long after this that Jackie found herself sitting across a tea table from one of the most powerful Triad bosses in the Walled City. He had become frustrated with the problem of addiction among his own followers. Although the Triads regularly dealt in drug trafficking, actual addiction often made their members useless to their gang. He amazingly proposed to give Jackie the addicts of his group to get them off drugs, but not budging, Jackie refused to help the young men break free of their heroin addiction only to return to their lives of violence and crime.

The leader then made her an offer never heard before; he told her that he would release from the Triad any of its members who wanted to follow Jesus. (Triad membership was always considered a lifetime commitment, and persons attempting to leave Triad membership often would be severely punished.) What an offer! What an opportunity for her Lord!

This arrangement gave Jackie an even greater "green light" for ministry to the drug addicts of the Walled City. She found that many of the people she helped among the addicted, poor, crippled, and homeless literally had nowhere to go and no way to start a new life. Eventually this led to the development of special homes for them and to the beginning of the St. Stephen's Society, which became actively involved in all aspects of help and rehabilitation to the people of Hong Kong who were in need of its services.

Jackie's one-woman crusade within the Walled City not only led to the development of a very successful drug rehabilitation program but also gave birth to an active, vibrant, Spirit-empowered church within the confines of the Walled City. Special group homes and ministries were developed, and ultimately, the government gave them facilities in which to continue their work and house the needy on a greater scale. These facilities became known as Hang Fook Camp, and they served as the base of operations for Jackie and the St. Stephen's Society for several years. But her emphasis was the preaching of the cross, holy abandonment to God, and the power of prayer.[4]

Jackie Pullinger-To is a warrior with the spiritual DNA of David and his mighty men. She was willing to leave the comforts of life in England to serve her divine purpose among the broken ones inside the Walled City of Hong Kong. Her purpose was fueled by a flame of passion—a passion so compelling that she refused to allow failure or obstacles to deter her from fulfilling her vision.

What through strength fails?
Boldness is certain to win praise.

In mighty enterprises, it is enough
to have had the determination.

—*Sextus Propertius*

CHAPTER SEVEN

POSSESSING YOUR TERRITORY— DETERMINATION

OR THOUSANDS OF YEARS, WARS have been waged over land. Geography has always been important in the history of man. Where you are living often determines what you are producing. If you live in a desert, you will not be able to produce a luscious garden. If you are living in the frigid north, you will not be growing citrus fruit. Who we are and what we do is influenced by where we live. Geography is very important to the purposes of God and His plans for your life. Where you determine to stand will determine what you will do. What you are doing will determine what you will reap. What you reap will be your inheritance that is passed down to future generations. Your determination to succeed will influence those around you, and it all starts with geography.

We have looked at this verse in a previous chapter, but I revisit it here to point out the importance of geography to your destiny. *Next to him was Shammah son of Agee the Hararite. When the Philistines banded together at a place where there was a field full of lentils, Israel's troops fled from them. But Shammah took his stand in the middle of the field. He defended it and struck the Philistines down, and the Lord brought about a great victory* (2 Samuel 23:11, 12).

Now, what would make a man fight for a field full of beans? What would make you risk your life for such a seemingly insignificant plot of land? It's very simple. It was his land and his beans. If this is not your bean field, you don't care. But let somebody go after your beans, and let's see what you'll do. *Your destiny is directly located or attached to a geographic location, and that is where your blessing is.*

THE RHYTHM OF POSITION AND PURPOSE

It's very important to find out *where* you are supposed to be and *when* you are supposed to be there. Location is important and timing is everything! The Spirit of God moves in the earth with a certain rhythm that is in sync with Father's divine will for your life. There is synchronization, a certain harmony, and a rhythm of the beat as the Spirit of God moves in agreement with the ultimate purpose.

This harmony with timing is important to the purposes of God in your life. It is important that you get to where you need to be at the time you need to be there. The flow of finding your right place means that you will face a certain amount of opposition. The enemy will seek to keep you from reaching the place of destiny and influence for your life if he possibly can.

Whenever you face opposition, you must stand your ground because opposition offers the opportunity for victory. Without opposition there is no victory. Opposition, victory—failure, overcoming—conflict, triumph—this is the rhythm of life that eventually leads you to your promised land. It is extremely important that you understand the power of geography and learn how to live in your promised position.

> *"In that day I will restore David's fallen tent. I will repair its broken places, restore its ruins, and build it as it used to be, so that they may possess the remnant of Edom and all the nations that bear my name," declares the Lord, who will do these things. "The days are coming," declares the Lord, "when the reaper will be overtaken by the plowman and the planter by the one treading grapes. New wine will drip from the mountains and flow from all the hills. I will bring back my exiled people Israel; they will rebuild the ruined cities and live in them. They will plant vineyards and drink their wine; they will make gardens and eat their fruit. I will plant Israel in their own land, never again to be uprooted from the land I have given them," says the Lord your God.*
> —Amos 9:11-15

The prophet is declaring that before the farmer can get the seed in the ground, your harvest is going to be there. God will bless the land that He has given to you even when you have failed to live up to the promises. Though we fail, He does not fail. He is more committed to His purposes in your life than you are.

There is a perfect time—that time is now—when God will strategically plant His people in the fields that He has chosen, and He has promised that in those fields He will bring forth a harvest. With divine wisdom and in agreement with the ultimate purpose, God is intentionally placing His people in the marketplaces of the world so that He can bring forth His kingdom.

Perhaps you have not fully understood that your fortune resides in the place of your destiny. Unfortunately, a huge percentage of people are working in the wrong occupation. They are mispositioned. Maybe they are doing what their parents did or what people expected them to do. But they experience neither peace nor blessing because they are in the wrong place at the wrong time. Let your passion guide you to your purpose. Listen to the rhythm of your heart and respond to that passionate beat. Positioning to God is everything, and you must get in the right place.

When you are in the right place, there is no toil, no worry, and no sweat. Will you have to work? Yes. But it will be with a great measure of peace and a huge portion of joy. God is restoring David's tabernacle, and his people will be planted in their land. They will not be uprooted. They will not be intimidated out of their harvest. They will not be pushed aside. But before this can happen, you must stand your ground like Shammah, and refuse to let anyone take the field that God has given to you.

GOD AND GEOGRAPHY

What is the big deal about geography, and is it important in Scripture? The word *earth* is mentioned in the Bible 906 times. The word *field* or *fields* is mentioned 324 times. The word *ground* is mentioned 188 times. But watch this: the word *land* is mentioned 1,489 times in Scripture. Is geography important to God? Yes it is. What do we mean by geography? *Geography* is the science that deals with description, distribution, and dealings of the diverse features of the earth's surface.

We will find some important revelation on this subject in the Book of Beginnings. *Genesis* means "the beginning or the origin," and it is there that geography is created. The first mention of land is found in Genesis, chapter 1. All of the creative actions of God—the reconciliation, restoration, reformation, everything that has to do with life and salvation, and the whole life of Christ—is depicted in the book of Genesis. If you read Genesis through the eyes of revelation, you will see Christ crucified many times and resurrected: Abraham and Isaac, the ram and the bush, and the third-day resurrection of land, which we are about to discuss. It can be found throughout the book. *Genesis is the blueprint for life.* It is God's architectural drawing.

The creation of man and woman, the creation of the garden, life before the fall, then the fall of man, and the atonement of man—all of this is revealed in the book of Genesis.

And God said, "Let the water under the sky be gathered to one place, and let dry ground appear." And it was so. God called the dry ground "land," and the gathered waters he called "seas." And God saw that it was good. Then God said, "Let the land produce vegetation: seed-bearing plants and trees on the land that bear fruit with seed in it, according to their various kinds." And it was so. The land produced vegetation: plants bearing seed according to their kinds and trees bearing fruit with seed in it

according to their kinds. And God saw that it was
good.

—Genesis 1:9-12

What does *appear* mean? The land appeared. The meaning for the word *appear* in the Hebrew is: "To arise or be discerned, to be obvious, to be seen or to be recognized." Let the dry land appear. In the next line the word *appear* also means "to make to enjoy or to have an experience." *So God brought land in order to create an experience.* The land did not appear until the waters were gathered. The land, the experience, the enjoyment, the discernment, the resurrection—none of it happened until the waters were gathered together in one place.

Verse 9 says, let the waters be gathered. The word *gathered* means "bound together, to bind together by twisting or by collecting." So, in essence, God said all the waters are going to be collected, bound up, and twisted together in one place.

GOD SETS BOUNDARIES

Proverbs 8:29 says, *he gave the sea its boundary so the waters would not overstep his command, and…he marked out the foundations of the earth.* The next verse goes on to say that wisdom was right there with Him. Does the Bible really say that God set a boundary for the waters? It does. He set a boundary for the waters and told them not to overstep their boundary. On the earth's surface today 70 percent of the earth's surface is water and only 30 percent is land. There is enough water on the face of the earth to cover its entire surface with a depth of two miles deep.

Over in Jeremiah 5:22, we find a word from the Lord: *"Should you not fear me?" declares the Lord. "Should you not tremble in my presence? I made the sand a boundary for the sea, an ever-lasting barrier it cannot cross. The waves may roll, but they cannot prevail; they may roar, but they cannot cross it."* God raised the land, and then He set a decree to protect what He had raised.

Naturally speaking, you might say that water has dominion because there is more water than land. But God says that the power of the depth of the water will be controlled, bound by the land. It cannot cover what He has resurrected, what He has raised up. When God has established a certain principle in the earth, it cannot be violated. You can theologize it, you can philosophize it, you can manipulate it, but you cannot change it. When God says this is how it's going to be, then that is how it is going to be.

When God set the boundaries of the sea, He set the tide. It comes in and goes out. And when the tide comes in, it looks intimidating. But it can only go so far because the Law has been set for water. God said, "You can come this far, but you can't go any further." There are certainly times when floods and hurricanes will cause the water to go beyond its boundary, but God's Law is inescapable, and eventually the waters will return to *their place.*

Seas often represent trouble in life. If you get this revelation, then you'll understand more clearly the principle of the following story. Jesus was sleeping in the boat as the disciples were guiding it across the water. A raging storm had developed, and the disciples were fretting about water in the boat, when Jesus awakened, looked at the sea, and said, "Peace." He looked at the disciples and said, "Be still," and the water calmed down. Jesus had power over the waters because He knew what their place was.

There was a boundary set for the waters, and Jesus simply enforced that boundary. Though a tempest of trouble should arise in your life, it only takes a word from the one who understands boundaries to command that storm to pass. No matter what your circumstances look like, there is a boundary. There is a Law in place that says it can beat against you and come upon you, but it cannot overtake you. "Storm, there's a boundary on you. You can only go so far."

David understood this truth. *He set the earth on its foundations; it can never be moved. You covered it with the deep as with a garment* (Psalm 104:5,6). In the creation of the world, God set fixed boundaries and established certain laws. Those who don't know God call this nature. But we who have experienced the power of His love in our lives know Him as the Creator of all things. He fixed boundaries between the land and the water and between the day and the night, so that we would understand that even though changes come into our lives, we can always find our way back to the borders that God has fixed for our lives.

Things might get dark in your life and the waters just might overflow their boundaries, but know this—God will roll back the waters and cause the light of His presence to cast away the darkness. David put it this way, *…weeping may endure for a night, but joy cometh in the morning* (Psalm 30:5 KJV). This is an immutable law of life. If there is nighttime there has to be daytime. If the floods come in and overflow our lives, they will eventually recede, and God's love will prevail over all that the enemy does.

THE THIRD DAY—THE DAY OF GOD

When did land appear? It was on the third day. God has established the principle of the third day. David was anointed in Hebron on the third day. Jesus turned water into wine at the wedding at Cana in Galilee. On what day? The third day. When did Esther go before the king? The third day. How long was Jonah in the belly of the whale? Three days. What day did Jesus get up out of the grave? The third day. What day did land appear? The third day. What millennium are we entering into? The third.

The power of three is found throughout the Scriptures: Outer court, Holy Place, Most Holy Place—spirit, soul, and body—faith, hope, and love—Father, Son, and Holy Spirit. On the third day the land appeared, and based upon the power of three, this act is important in the purposes of God.

Second Peter 3:8 says that a thousand years is like a day and a day is like a thousand years with the Lord. So if we count forward from the center of God's purposes—the crucifixion— then we are entering into the third day, which is the third millennium. Something good is about to happen for you. Your land is about ready to appear above the face of the waters. God has set boundaries for the blessings that He wants to give to you. God wants you to be established—spiritually, emotionally, mentally, financially, and professionally.

In Genesis God called the dry land earth. In the Hebrew, the word *earth* is translated: "to be firmed or to be established." On the third day, God unveiled the place where His purposes would be established. He unveiled something that was firm and immoveable. On the third day, God said, "I'm going to reveal to My creation that thing which is established and cannot be shaken."

God unveiled what was already there. He simply rolled back the waters and uncovered the earth that already existed. There is a purpose for the earth, and He unveiled the land so that He could unveil His purpose. *And God said, Let the earth bring forth grass, the herb yielding seed, and the fruit tree yielding fruit after his kind, whose seed is in itself, upon the earth: and it was so. And the earth brought forth grass, and herb yielding seed after his kind, and the tree yielding fruit, whose seed was in itself, after his kind: and God saw that it was good* (Genesis 1:11,12 KJV).

BORN TO REPRODUCE

What is the purpose of the land? The purpose of the land is for reproduction. Land is commanded by the voice of God to produce. God produced the land in such a way that it would bring forth the very seed that would reproduce the grass, the trees, and the flowers of the earth. Life was in the dust of the earth.

What did God form you out of? He took the dust of the earth and shaped you into a being, and then he breathed into you celestial fluid (God's breath), and you became a living being. Already within you is the seed for reproducing God's purpose in the earth. You don't need to wait on God for some magical gift. He created you in His image, redeemed you by His blood, and made you able to reproduce His life in yourself and in others. Who you are influences others and has the power of reproducing your character, your attitudes, and your thoughts in other people. This is the power of influence.

When God created Adam, He gave him a parcel of ground called Eden. *Now the Lord God had planted a garden in the east, in Eden; and there he* put *the man he had formed* (Genesis 2:8). God placed (*sum* in Hebrew, meaning "assigned, ordained, established") Adam in the garden. This was the place God had ordained for Adam. He created a special environment for Adam so that he could fulfill his purpose in that place. Further down, in verse 15, we see a second form of the word *placed* or *put*.

The Lord God took the man and put *him in the Garden of Eden to work it and take care of it.* The word used here is different from the one in verse 8. In Hebrew, the word for *put* is *nuach,* which has an interesting meaning: "deposited, rested and positioned." God put Adam in the garden expecting that as he fulfilled his purpose, God would earn interest on His deposit in the land. The land should be better off after Adam has cultivated, worked, and cared for it. In other words, anywhere that God places you should be better off when you leave it than when you found it.

The life of God in you should recreate His life wherever you go. This is the power of influence. Your relationships with others should enrich their lives. Your work at your job should increase the effectiveness of that company. God has placed His life within your spirit and wherever you go, you should impact others.

DON'T CURSE YOUR GROUND

As we drift over into chapter 3, we watch Adam and Eve forfeit their ground through disobedience, and this insubordination will curse the ground that belonged to them. Ultimately, they will be driven away from their holy ground that became cursed.

Through his subtle words to mesmerize Eve, the serpent was able to seduce her to the dark side. Unwilling to abide alone in this dark place, Eve went to Adam and enticed him to sin. Both ended up in the darkness. Standing alone in the darkness, they heard a voice penetrating their naked place. It is the voice of God, "Adam, where are you?" He knew where Adam was. He's

God. Adam didn't know where Adam was. God is the master of asking just the right questions.

His questions pierce the hardened walls that we construct through our disobedience, and He exposes us to ourselves. The thing to remember about the questions of God is that questions unveil our sin so that He can heal our sin. Religious men question so that they can expose and condemn. God questions so that He can reveal and heal.

It is essential to note the cause of the fall. Satan caused Adam and Eve to doubt God's Word. Faith is the most powerful force in the world. But faith transformed into doubt will cause our world to fall apart. Look at the curse that came on Adam in Genesis 3:17-19, *To Adam he said, "Because you listened to your wife and ate from the tree about which I commanded you, 'You must not eat of it,' cursed is the ground because of you; through painful toil you will eat of it all the days of your life. It will produce thorns and thistles for you, and you will eat the plants of the field. By the sweat of your brow you will eat your food until you return to the ground, since from it you were taken; for dust you are and to dust you will return."*

The land is cursed and man is robbed of his rest. He will now sweat as he works in the cursed field. The land that was to be a blessing has now become a curse.

REVERSING THE CURSE AND FINDING YOUR WAY HOME

The great wonder of the love and majesty of God is that He did not leave us in our cursed place. He became a curse on a tree so that He could redeem man from his cursed place and bring him back into his inheritance. Atonement took you out of the land of thorns and thistles and put you in the land of grace and glory, bounty and blessing.

There is an inheritance waiting for you if you can find your way back to the blessed land that God has for you. Jesus showed the way when He declared that the meek would inherit the earth in Matthew 5:5. The ways of God are not the ways of man, and the way back is not through the ingenuity of man's genius or the strength of man's might.

God employs the weak and simple of this world to reclaim the land that has been lost. In that place there is prosperity and healing waiting for you. But like Abram you will have to get up and leave the land where you are and go to the land that has been promised to you. Sometimes you don't know where you are going. I have noticed that sometimes God is not very specific when He gives you a word.

What do you do? You just get up and go until you hear Him say, "Stop." You will never know what great things await you until you walk unto a land that He has prepared for you. God wanted to make of Abram a great nation, but it would never happen until he found the land where it could happen.

When you get in place—into your position—geographically situated in the location that God has for you, then God will be able to release His blessing on you. It will come back to you on every wave. Everything you do will be blessed. You won't be able to do anything that doesn't succeed. Everything you touch will prosper. When you possess your territory you unlock an inheritance of blessings and favor.

CHARACTER SKETCH—
DETERMINATION

Martin Luther King, Jr.

MARTIN LUTHER KING, JR. WAS born on January 15, 1929. King grew up in the South under an oppressive, intolerant system of racial laws called Jim Crow laws. These laws were a political and social manifestation of deep racial hatred and prejudice. This prejudice, entrenched for generations, had economically enhanced the lives of a few while it robbed the soul of a whole nation. This system created a barrier, a separation of blacks from the whites, that required the blacks to drink at different water fountains, use different washrooms, ride in different sections of buses and trains, visit different recreational facilities and parks, and live in different communities. It was against these laws and social prejudice that the determined Martin would wage a holy war of nonviolence. Surrounded by political and society pressures from all sides, Martin Luther King, Jr. was determined to stand up for what was right, and to do so in the right way.

Martin attended public schools in Georgia that were still strictly segregated. At the age of fifteen he graduated from high school and then went off to attend Morehouse College in Atlanta (both his grandfather and father graduated from Morehouse). He graduated in 1948 from Morehouse, and then three years later received a Bachelor of Divinity from Crozier Theological Seminary in Pennsylvania. Continuing his education in 1955, he went to Boston University where he went on to receive a Ph.D in Theology. It was there that he met and married Coretta Scott.

Reverend King was pastor of the Dexter Avenue Baptist Church in Montgomery, Alabama, from 1954 to 1959. In November 1959, he resigned the pastorate and moved to Atlanta to take leadership of the Southern Christian Leadership Conference. He was president of the Southern Christian Leadership Conference until his death as well as co-pastor at Ebenezer Baptist Church.

Martin's convictions of equality for all men grew and in December of 1955, he became a key leader in one of the first nonviolent political demonstrations in the United States, the Montgomery Bus Boycott. During the Montgomery Bus Boycott, blacks boycotted the city buses until they were allowed to sit in any seat, instead of having to move to the back when a white was on board.

It was during the days of boycott that King was arrested, his home was bombed, and he suffered personal abuse. Even in the midst of all the personal turmoil, Martin Luther King, Jr. was beginning to step onto the world stage and be recognized for his leadership ability and determination for equal rights. He received the Nobel Peace Prize at the age of 35, the youngest ever to do so, and donated the proceeds to the cause.

Martin Luther King, Jr. was one who fought with determination for the God-given rights that every man, woman, and child were born with. He was out to possess the territory that had been forbidden to his people.

Martin Luther King, Jr's life was cut short when on April 4, 1968, King was shot by James Earl Ray in Memphis, Tennessee. He was only 39 at the time of his tragic death. Dr. King was getting ready to turn his focus towards a nationwide campaign to help the poor. That effort would be cut short by his assassination. "He had never wavered in his insistence that nonviolence must remain the central tactic of the civil-rights movement, nor in his faith that everyone in America would some day attain equal justice."[1]

Dr. King lived his life fighting for what he believed in. He believed that a man should not be judged by the color of his skin but by his character. His determination for truth and right cost him his life, and opened the doors for a powerful inheritance for succeeding generations. His dream for America, birthed in determination, became the dream of a nation.

I have a dream that one day on the red hills of Georgia, sons of former slaves and sons of former slave owners will be able to sit down together at the table of brotherhood. ...

I have a dream my four little children will one day live in a nation where they will not be judged by the color of their skin but by content of their character. I have a dream today! [2]

— Martin Luther King, Jr.,
"I Have a Dream"

Human progress never rolls in on wheels of inevitability. It comes through the tireless efforts and persistent work of men willing to be co-workers with God, and without this hard work, time itself becomes an ally of the forces of social stagnation.[3]

—Martin Luther King, Jr.,
"Letter from Birmingham City Jail"

At that moment I experienced the presence of the Divine as I had never before experienced him. It seemed as though I could hear the quiet assurance of an inner voice, saying, "Stand up for righteousness, stand up for truth. God will be at your side forever." Almost at once my fears began to pass from me. My uncertainty disappeared. I was ready to face anything. The outer situation remained the same, but God had given me inner calm.[4]

—Martin Luther King, Jr.

I still believe that standing up for the truth of God is the greatest thing in the world. This is the end of life. The end of life is not to be happy. The end of life is not to achieve pleasure and avoid pain. The end of life is to do the will of God, come what may.[5]

—Martin Luther King, Jr.,
"The Most Durable Power"

In necessary things, unity;
in doubtful things, liberty;
in all things, charity.

—Richard Baxter

Chapter Eight

Building a Dynasty—Unity

OR THREE YEARS JESUS HAD been a spiritual teacher, a mentor, to a group of twelve men. These twelve men were not extraordinary men. In fact, they were very ordinary men. His teaching was not simply by instruction, but through His words. It was also by impartation, through His life.

As Jesus was facing His final and ultimate task for man—His death, burial, and resurrection—He gathered them together in the Upper Room. There He told them that it was expedient for them that He go to the Father because if He didn't leave them then the comforter or the counselor could not come (see John 14:16-21).

He concluded this thought by saying that the result of His departure and the coming of the Holy Spirit would be that His band of men would do greater works than He had done. In order to understand what Jesus was saying in that statement, you must understand that He was not speaking in terms of *dynamic* but in terms of *dimension*.

DYNAMIC, DIMENSION, AND DYNASTY

It is not so much an issue of imitating His dynamic but increasing His dimension, His sphere, His influence, His capacity to reach the whole world. Rather than the power of God being manifested through His unique Son, it would now be expressed through a whole family, creating a dynasty of men and women who reflect His nature and who have His power.

The dimension of the work would be greater because Jesus was going to empower a team of people. When Jesus came, He did not choose one person to succeed Him, but He very specifically chose a team of twelve men to carry on what He had started. In the book of Acts, chapter two, we find those twelve men receiving the authority and power that He promised them would come. That power would then be extended to hundreds and then thousands, and it would reach forward into future generations.

So Jesus left a dynasty that was created by the integration and the interconnection between the individual destinies of His people. It is important for you to understand that you have a very specific assignment, a destiny that God has called you to fulfill. He gave you the anointing—the divine ability to complete that assigned task. But life cannot be lived within the context of our individual destinies.

It must be lived within a greater purpose and environment. That greater environment is the dynasty—the connecting of our lives with others who also have a destiny and an anointing to fulfill that destiny. Jesus did not leave one man to succeed Him. He left a team of people to complete what He had started.

In Isaiah 9:7, the prophet declared that of the increase of His (the coming Messiah) dynasty (government; kingdom), there would be no end. Exponentially, through the combination of destinies that have been linked together, God's kingdom would continue to fill the earth.

The word *destiny* means "something to which a person is called to do—a predetermined plan and course that is prepared for one's live." God does have a wonderful plan for your life.

Dynasty is a succession of rulers, a sequence of kings, and a series of ruling families that succeed into future generations. Dynasty also is a powerful group or family that maintains its position for a considerable time.

Destiny has more to do with *me,* while dynasty has more to do with *us.* Destiny is where *I* am going; dynasty is where *we* are going. Destiny is my place in the earth but dynasty is where my destiny is connected to your destiny, and we are going together.

IMPOSTERS AND INTRUDERS

Then thou spakest in vision to thy holy one, and saidst, I have laid help upon one that is mighty; I have exalted one chosen out of the people. I have found David my servant; with my holy oil have I anointed him: With whom my hand shall be established: mine arm also shall strengthen him. The enemy shall not exact upon him; nor the son of wickedness afflict him. And I will beat down his foes before his face, and plague them that hate him. But my faithfulness and my mercy shall be with him: and in my name shall his horn be exalted. I will set his hand also in the sea, and his right hand in the rivers. He shall cry unto me. Thou art my father, my God, and the rock of my salvation. Also I will make him my firstborn, higher than the kings of the earth. My mercy will I keep for him for evermore, and my covenant shall stand fast with him. His seed also will I make to endure for ever, and his throne as the days of heaven.

—Psalm 89:19-29 KJV

Verses 28 and 29 declare that God will establish a dynasty through the lineage of David—a succession of rulers of the same lineage, the same family. It was the plan of God that His ultimate purposes would be established through the dynasty of David. God brought him to the throne and then gave him a family that would extend his life through succeeding generations.

Along the way there would be intruders and imposters. *Then king Solomon sware by the Lord, saying, God do so to me, and more also, if Adonijah have not spoken this word against his own life. Now therefore, as the Lord liveth, which hath established me, and set me on the throne of David my father, and who hath made me an house, as he promised. Adonijah shall be put to death this day. And king Solomon sent by the hand of Benaiah the son of Jehoiada; and he fell upon him that he died* (1 Kings 2:23-25).

David chose his son Solomon as his successor to inherit the dynasty. His half-brother Adonijah proceeded with plots and schemes to insure that he was crowned as David's successor. His conspiracy, however, was blocked by the prophet Nathan, who rushed to have David and Bathsheba approve a timely coronation for their beloved son Solomon. Although Adonijah pledged loyalty to Solomon, Solomon quickly became alarmed at Adonijah's bold and somewhat treasonous request to marry Abishag, David's nurse. Solomon knew that in order to preserve the dynasty, Adonijah must die. He could have been there alongside of Solomon, but because he tried to usurp the throne, he lost his opportunity to be at the king's side. Everyone has a place that they are to fill, but we must beware of the danger of taking the place of another. We are gifted and anointed for our place—not the place of another.

UNITY OF VISION

It is our destiny to create a dynasty. How do we secure our dynasty in the earth? God has anointed and gifted us so that together we might establish His kingdom in all the earth. In order to secure a dynasty, we must first have *unity of vision*. Now, here is a truth you must grab hold of. When we are able to link all of our abilities, talents, and energies into a synchronized effort to build the vision of God in the house of God, then God will be sure that your personal vision for your family is also established.

David's mighty men never forsook him. They were loyal to him, and when he got to the throne they got there as well. His victory became their victory and secured a blessing for their families. We have talked so much about generational curses, but somebody forgot to tell us about generational blessings. Your blessings can become an inheritance for your family and future generations.

Vince Lombardi, one of the greatest football coaches of all time, once said: "Build for your team a feeling of oneness, of dependence on one another, and of strength to be derived by unity."[1] There is a strength that comes from unity that you can't find in yourself. There's a strength that can be derived from a team that you can't get individually. Vince Lombardi under-stood what Jesus taught. Nothing can break the power of unity.

DIVERSITY EMBRACED IS UNITY ACHIEVED

If the whole football team consisted of quarterbacks, you would not have a team. You would have a group of quarterbacks. Diversity embraced is unity achieved. Unity achieved is power released. And power released will result in people changed. When we talk about embracing unity, we are talking about the other side of the unity coin.

Unity is not uniformity. We are not talking about imitation but a unity that is based upon the mutual respect and embrace of the gifts of one another. *The body is a unit, though it is made up of many parts; and though all its parts are many, they form one body. So it is with Christ. For we were all baptized by one Spirit into one body—whether Jews or Greeks, slave or free—and we were all given the one Spirit to drink. Now the body is not made up of one part but of many* (1 Corinthians 12:12-14).

God created us all differently. We have different personali-ties. We have different motivations. We have different abilities. And it is these differences that make us unique. God's great joy is to create a unity out of those differences. In order to do that, in Hebrew we must be able to appreciate how God has created others. We must respect who they are and what they do.

An independent spirit will destroy the power of unity. Unity's foundation is constructed from humility, submissive-ness, gentleness, respect, and reverence for others. So in Christ we who are many are created to form one unit, a body, and we belong to one another.

We genuinely care for each other. That's how you build a dynasty. We know how to place individual rights beneath the best interest of the team. *Individualism wins trophies, but team-work builds dynasties.*

Jesus didn't leave a successor—He left a team—and this team is willing to pay the price that will bring the victory. In order to build a dynasty, there must be sacrifice. All success is built on the back of sacrifice and pain. The dynasty of God—His kingdom—will come when His gifted people join their hearts together in a unity of purpose and are willing to pay the price to secure that victory.

THE TRIBES OF GOD DEMONSTRATE THE DYNASTY OF GOD

One of the key principles concerning a dynasty is that it is composed of tribes. The tribes of Israel made up the kingdom of Israel. There cannot be any dynasty without tribes.

> *I was glad when they said unto me, Let us go into the house of the Lord. Our feet shall stand within thy gates, O Jerusalem. Jerusalem is builded as a city that is compact together: Whither the tribes go up, the tribes of the Lord, unto the testimony of Israel, to give thanks unto the name of the Lord. For there are set thrones of judgment, the thrones of the house of David. Pray for the peace of Jerusalem: they shall prosper that love thee. Peace is within thy walls, and prosperity within thy palaces. For my brethren and companions' sakes, I will now say, Peace be within thee. Because of the house of the Lord our God I will seek thy good.*
>
> —Psalm 122:1-9 KJV

This was a song of ascent, a song sung by the Jewish pilgrims as they ascended up to the city of Jerusalem. Jerusalem was the capital of the Jewish nation and the center of their worship, for it was in Jerusalem that the temple was built—the temple that housed the Ark of the Covenant, the place of His Presence.

This is what it means to be Israel—gathered together for worship and service of their God. All the people of Israel, the Lord's people, make their pilgrimage here. They come to give thanks to the name of the Lord as the law requires. Here stand the thrones where judgment is given—the thrones of the dynasty of David.

Where did the tribes come from? They came from sons—the sons of Jacob. All tribes relate back to Abraham but have their distinction from the sons of Jacob. There is unity and diversity among the different tribes. They are all sons of Abraham—that is their unity. They are descended from different sons of Jacob—that is their diversity.

The word *tribe* means "a plan or means to branch off, or a branch of." It would be as if you would take a tree and there would be a limb going this way and that limb would branch out to the right or branch out to the left. That would be the family tree and each tribe had their particular branch. All are of the same tree, but branch off in different directions. The tribe was the major social unit that comprised the makeup of a nation.

The tribe was comprised of what was referred to as *clans*. The *clan* was a family, families, or a cluster of households that had a common ancestry. The clan was then comprised of the individual household or families referred to as the father's house. So then we can say a tribe is a collection of families descending from one common ancestor.

The tribes live separately and function together as a unique family different from others, but whenever the trumpets are sounded for either war or for worship, the tribes will become a nation. If the work of God is to become a dynasty, we must learn to function as tribes. There is a time to be off doing what God has called us to do, but when the prophetic trumpet sounds, we know how to drop the plow and gather together with all of God's people.

THE TESTIMONY OF THE PEOPLE

> *Whither the tribes go up, the tribes of the Lord, unto the testimony of Israel, to give thanks unto the name of the Lord. For there are set thrones of judgment, the thrones of the house of David.*
>
> —Psalm 122:4,5 KJV

It was the rule in Israel to praise the Lord in Jerusalem. The tribes would ascend unto the city of God to give witness to their commitment to the God of Israel. This was their testimony—it was recorded in songs of worship and praise. *Testimony* means "an outward sign or an open acknowledgement or public confession." They were going to Jerusalem with purpose and timing.

There is a *when* and a *why* to going to the house of the Lord. When we go to the house of the Lord, we declare or make a profession to others. When we go to the house of God, we make an open declaration concerning our relationship with Him.

The testimony is a statute, a rule, a principle, and a decree. It is a decree and principle that David's dynasty lived by. The principle that we live by is that when it is time for the tribes to go up, we don't miss it. Every dynasty must have a testimony—principles by which they live that distinguish them from other people. It is their unique representation to the world declaring who they are, what they stand for, and where they are going.

God gave us a recipe for success in our lives. He said if we will do it like He tells us to, we will have guaranteed prosperity and success. And this is just one principle out of hundreds of principles in Scripture to prove the point that our prosperity is not in our wealth, but in the blessing of God on our lives that only comes through obedience to the principles.

That testimony must be clear and distinct so that it does not create confusion in the minds of those who are walking in obedience to the principles together. Each one of us is called to uniquely testify to the reality of Jesus Christ through the lives that we live in this world.

THERE IS NO SUCCESSOR
IF THERE IS NO SUCCESS

In The New Living Translation, Psalm 122:5 reads like this: *Here stand the thrones where judgment is given, the thrones of the dynasty of David.* When you think of a dynasty, you think of winning. You think of success, not failure. There can be no successor if there is not first a measure of success, victory, and accomplishment. You cannot give anything until something has been given to you. David had something to give to succeeding generations because God gave something to him. Second Samuel discusses the establishment of David's dynasty:

> *After the king was settled in his palace and the Lord had given him rest from all his enemies around him, he said to Nathan the prophet, "Here I am, living in*

*a palace of cedar, while the ark of God remains in
a tent." Nathan replied to the King, "Whatever you
have in mind, go ahead and do it for the Lord is
with you." That night, the word of the Lord came to
Nathan, saying: "Go and tell my servant David, 'This
is what the Lord says: Are you the one to build me a
house to dwell in? I have not dwelt in a house from
the day I brought the Israelites up out of Egypt to this
day. I have been moving from place to place with a
tent as my dwelling. Wherever I have moved with
all the Israelites, did I ever say to any of their rulers
whom I commanded to shepherd my people Israel,
"Why have you not built me a house of cedar?"'*

*"Now then, tell my servant David, 'This is what
the Lord Almighty says: I took you from the pasture
and from following the flock to be ruler over my
people Israel. I have been with you wherever you
have gone, and I have cut off all your enemies from
before you. Now I will make your name great, like
the names of the greatest men of the earth. And I
will provide a place for my people Israel and will
plant them so that they can have a home of their
own and no longer be disturbed. Wicked people will
not oppress them anymore, as they did at the beginning and have done ever since the time I appointed
leaders over my people Israel. I will also give you rest
from all your enemies. The Lord declares to you that
the Lord himself will establish a house for you.'"*

—2 Samuel 7:1-11

David wanted to do something for God, but God wanted to do something for David. God made it clear to David (beginning in verse 12) that when his days were over, He would raise up an offspring to succeed him whose kingdom would be established forever. This offspring would come from David's own body, but God would establish his kingdom. He was the one who would build a house for David's family—a dynasty.

Just as God chose David, He has chosen you and given to you a measure of grace and gifting that will create a succession in your life. He came looking for you when you were not desiring Him. He pursued His plan for your life when you did not know there was a plan. He placed His riches in your hands so that you can bless others and create your own succession.

Your success with what God has given you will be determined by your commitment to the destiny that will be part of a dynasty. Unfortunately, too many of us never get around to pursuing that dream. Procrastination is the leading cause of failure. There is a time to be patient, but there is also a time to be aggressive and pursue the success that God has promised to you.

GOD'S COMMITMENT TO YOU IS HIS PRESENCE WITH YOU!

Look again at 2 Samuel 7:9, *"I have been with you wherever you have gone, and I have cut off all your enemies from before you. Now I will make your name great, like the names of the greatest men in the earth."*

God's commitment to you is guaranteed by His presence with you. As Jesus stood on the mountain preparing to make His departure, He promised His disciples that He would be with them. The key to your success does not lie with you—it lies with God's presence with you. That's why Moses on the mountain insisted that God's presence go with Israel. He was not going to take one single step unless he could negotiate and secure the fact that God would go with them.

His presence seeks your presence every day of the week. If you never get another miracle, money, a new car, or whatever it is that you are seeking, the one thing you should desire with all of your heart is that when you get out of bed in the morning you know with all of your heart that God is with you.

We know that when the presence of God is there grace is available. Grace is a manifestation of mercy. Grace is an act of mercy. Grace is the *activation* of mercy. God's presence brings His mercy and His grace. Paul declared that whatever He was, He was by the grace of God. Grace is favor and *favor* means success.

The presence of God separates us from all of the other people in the earth, making us a unique and special people. There is a significant difference between those who experience His presence and those who do not. There is a certain aware-ness, a special aroma, and a unique poise that is attached to those who have His presence.

DO YOU HAVE YOUR KEYS?

There is an innate ability in the dynasty to figure out the combi-nation of components that gives you access to control your possession and success in all areas of your life. The man with the keys is the man with control. You can own your house, but if you lose your keys, you can't get in. There's nothing more frustrating than being locked out of your own possession. And for too long too many people have been locked out of their promise.

God wants to restore to you all that has been lost, and He has placed keys into your hands that will help you regain your lost possessions. When you have the **master key,** there is nothing that you can be locked out of if it belongs to you. If it is your possession, then God has given you a master key to get you into the place that He has prepared for you. Here is the master key—*revelation*. *Revelation* is your passage into the lineage. The only way for a person to get into this dynasty is to have a revelation of who Jesus Christ is and an understanding of who you are in Him.

The power of revelation is the ability to see something that you have been looking at for a long time but have never seen. Revelation is a gift from God. It is the Holy Spirit who was sent by the Father so He would guide us into all truth. Revelation is an unveiling of truth. You *see* truth before you *know* truth. Revelation is enlightened understanding.

Paul, writing to the church of Ephesus, prayed that the eyes of our understanding would be enlightened. It is possible to read but not understand what you are reading. But when the light of revelation shines into your spirit, then you can see, and with seeing comes understanding. This is one of the great keys of those who belong to the dynasty of God—they get revelation.

Bible colleges and seminaries can give you knowledge, but they cannot give you revelation. That comes from God. Matthew 13:19 says, *"When anyone hears the message about the kingdom and does not understand it, the evil one comes and snatches away what was sown in his heart."* If you don't understand it, you'll lose it. That's what He just said, but verse 23 says he that receives seed into *"...good soil is the man who hears the word and understands it...."* The individual who receives revelation and understands it is the one who will bear fruit, yielding a hundred, sixty, or thirty times what was sown.

In the New Testament book of Matthew, we find an excellent example of revelation realized by the disciple Peter:

> *When Jesus came to the region of Caesarea Philippi, he asked his disciples, "Who do people say the Son of Man is?" They replied, "Some say John the Baptist; others say Elijah; and still others, Jeremiah or one of the prophets." "But what about you?" he asked. "Who do you say I am?" Simon Peter answered, "You are the Christ, the Son of the living God." Jesus replied, "Blessed are you, Simon son of Jonah, for this was not revealed to you by man, but by my Father in heaven. And I tell you that you are Peter, and on this rock I will build my church, and the gates of Hades will not overcome it. I will give you the keys of the kingdom of heaven; whatever you bind on earth will be bound in heaven, and whatever you loose on earth will be loosed in heaven."*
> —Matthew 16:13-19

Peter's revelation got him the keys. It is the revelation of Jesus Christ that is the master key. If you don't have that key, then there will be no blessing or succession.

Now, Peter didn't get that revelation in some school. It came to him through the power of the Holy Spirit. The Spirit shone a light into Peter's spirit so that he could see Christ and thus make this public declaration. Revelation is your transition from darkened understanding to enlightened understanding. So revelation puts you in the lineage—it comes by the Spirit. It is not what you say. It is what you understand.

CHARACTER SKETCH—UNITY

Alexander the Great

THE DICTIONARY DEFINES UNITY AS oneness. The portals of history have a way of defining one's impact or greatness by their ability or inability to unify people and situations. Alexander the Great truly lived up to his name by using his ability to unite men, kingdoms, and cultures. Unity starts at the top with the vision of the leader and his effective communication to those under his charge. Alexander had the vision, the communication skills, and the ability to inspire and motivate those committed to his vision. A leader cannot lead without the ability to motivate and inspire unity.

Alexander the Great is often acknowledged for his military feats in conquering much of what was then the civilized world. He was driven by his ambition to influence the world so it would reflect the culture and values of Macedonia. He truly believed that it was his destiny to unite (conquer) all of the separate tribes and kingdoms under one force of thought and greatness.

From his position as king of Macedonia, Alexander would become one of the greatest leaders in history, guided by his brash energy and fiery imagination. It wasn't just his conquests that led him to greatness. Alexander not only went forth to conquer with the sword but to capture hearts and minds. It was through Alexander that the philosophies of Socrates and Plato spread to the world, embedding Greek thought and philosophy in every aspect of life—creating such a powerful impact that it is still reflected in the landscape and thought of those cultures and lands thousands of years later.

Alexander's greatness and desire to unify the world was infused into him from birth. Born in 356 BC, his father, Philip of Macedon, worked his whole life to unify the people of Macedonia and the tribes of Greece. One of Philip's first steps of unity was his marriage to Alexander's mother, Olympias who was not Macedonian but from what was considered a foreign land.

"...Alexander had a distinguished inheritance from both his parents. He combined the best qualities of Philip and Olympias; from his father came his sober judgment, clear intellect, reliable, systematic and practical methods of work; from his mother was derived his passionate, warm-hearted, romantic, emotional nature."[2]

Philip, Alexander's father, was described by Isocrates, a Greek philosopher of his time, as a leader and king who understood that generosity gained more co-operation from foes than destruction and tyranny.[3]

At the age of thirteen, Alexander became the student of one of the greatest philosophers of all times—Aristotle. Young Alexander was possessed with an eagerness to learn everything he could. From the beginning, there was a sense of destiny upon his life, and he knew that knowledge and experience would take him to the places he needed to go. Aristotle was impressed with the young mind of Alexander and fed him daily doses of great Grecian literature.

Not only did young Alexander develop his mind, but he also developed his body through sports and daily exercise. It was Aristotle who opened up the eyes of Alexander to the countries and cultures of the world. Of course, he also had the advantage of being the son of a great king, which gave him the opportunity to talk to ambassadors from other countries, as well as other famous people visiting the court of his father. It wasn't long until he had his first opportunity to go into war. At the age of eighteen, he was given the command of his father's cavalry.

When his father was assassinated, Alexander quickly moved to establish himself as king of Greece. The Greeks were not ready to accept his leadership, but one by one they either submitted to his leadership or were conquered by him. These men, who at first did not want to accept Alexander the Great, would go on to follow him for years, expanding the cause of unity from Asia Minor to Egypt, throughout the Persian Empire (the Middle East), and into much of present-day India.

To cover all the aspects and facts of Alexander's life that exemplify his leadership skills in unification would be a book in itself. One of the best examples of how his men and fellow comrades felt about him is expressed in an exchange of sentiment, after years of travel and conquest had kept them away from home and brought them into the heart of the Persian Empire. Tired, battle-worn, and homesick, many of the Macedonian men who had been with him from the beginning were on the verge of mutiny. Wounded in their hearts by Alexander's acceptance of many of the conquered Persians into the military ranks and into his inner circle, reconciliation came when they realized that his love and admiration for them had not diminished, but his acceptance (unity) of others had increased.

His ability to garner trust and motivate men to believe in something greater than themselves and to push on past self-sacrificing circumstances is shown during a battle in India known as the Millian campaign. Seeing that his men, under heavy assault, were losing the mind and vigor for war, Alexander thrust himself to the front of the battle lines, up a ladder, and into the enemy fortification.

"Standing with his back against the wall, fighting every man who dared approach, he slew several, including the leader of the enemy force. With his shield he protected his body from the arrows coming from every direction. When four of his foes had fallen, the Indians retired, but the missiles from the towers became more dangerous. By his side stood Peucestas, Leonnatus and Abreas, a corporal; presently, Abreas fell, pierced by an arrow. Then, suddenly, another arrow hit Alexander in the chest and penetrated to the lung. Blood flowed profusely from the wound, mingled with his breath; still he tried to fight on, but fell unconscious. Though also wounded and bleeding, Peucestas and Leonnatus stood over their King, guarding his body until some of the soldiers, maddened with rage and fear, with stakes and pegs clambered up the wall, and others forced a way through gates and breaches which they had hammered open. Terrified at the sight of Alexander, prostrate and bleeding, their ferocity knew no bounds; the slaughter was merciless."4

Alexander survived this battle wound as well as many others. Even though he was almost always significantly outnumbered and short on supplies, he won every battle he ever fought because of his ability to unify those around him.

His life ended far from his home in the hills of Macedonia when he died of Malaria in 323 BC, at the age of thirty-three, thirteen years after he became king. His life as a leader and historical figure was short, but the impact of his ability to unify men and win over cultures has survived for thousands of years. Alexander was considered great because of his ability to maintain and spread unity.

Destiny is not a matter of chance.
It is a matter of choice.
It is not a thing to be waited for.
It is a thing to be achieved.

Pastor Rick Hawkins

Conclusion

E ALL LIVE UNDER THE influence of other people, and we all have influence over other people. All men are a montage of other men, and our lives have been shaped by the varying influences that have drifted into our lives, whether they are dramatic or subtle in their approach.

Within the circle of influence, men must live by the power of covenant and friendship. Inside the bond of covenantal friendship, we will discover a new freedom and confidence to be who we were called to be. People who live in isolation from other people will eventually enter into the world of the weird and bizarre. Within our society, we consider a recluse as a person who is mentally unstable. It is not normal to live in isolation from others, and that kind of isolation will cripple our lives.

No one ever said that living within the circle of community would be easy. There will be times, as we have seen with David, that we might be forced to live in a cave rather than the palace. It is during those times of crisis that we will discover who are our real friends. It is during the times of trouble that friendships are born and the circle is either increased or decreased according to how the community walks through the minefields of misfortune.

Leadership is more effective when it is through the exercise of influence as opposed to the pressure of authority. People are more easily motivated by the influence of the life of the one *next to* them when compared to the insensitive imposition of power over them. They are deeply moved to action by the example of others. Albert Schweitzer once said that example is not the main thing in influencing others. It is the only thing. We influence people the best through our lives, more than our words.

As we have seen, when people are gathered together under the flag of purpose, they will follow the leader. Leaders who influence others will provide for people a sense of purpose and direction. As people gather together within the circle of purpose, a sense of destiny and unity will be created. It is within that circle of influence, where a people of unity have been created, that we have the greatest opportunity to change the world.

The Bible says in Matthew 11:12, "*And from the days of John the Baptist until now the kingdom of heaven suffereth violence and the violent take it by force*" (KJV). Three of the Greek words for violence are energy, might, and desperation. This is a desperate hour that must be matched with desperate people. A people that are energetic, mighty, and desperate will advance the kingdom of God in the last days. Their lives have been forged together in the blessing of living together as well as walking together through the fires of adversity.

This generation needs a new company of "mighty men." The Jewish prophet, Joel, prophetically declared in Joel 3:9, "*Wake up the mighty men*" (KJV).

I believe that we are living in that day. The mighty men and women of God are arising. They are coming up: they are drawing near.

Someone once said, "The kingdom of God is not for the well meaning, but for the one in whom the violence of devotion matches the desperation of the soul!"

May the violence of devotion match the desperation of our souls in this day. May our "inner circle," be strong, for we value friendship, trust, and influence.

NOTES

Chapter 1: The Power of *Next*—Influence

1. Henry Drummond, *The Greatest Thing in the World* (1880, 1920, Grand Rapids, MI: Christian Classics Ethereal Library), http://www.ccel.org/ccel/drummond/greatest.v.iii.html.

2. Ibid.

3. "Return to Pakistan Stadium," *Black Hawk Down*, DVD, Directed by Ridley Scott (Culver City, CA: Columbia Pictures, 2001).

4. Bible History online, "Ancient Babylonia—The Babylonian Captivity," http://www.bible-history.com/babylonia/BabyloniaThe_Babylonian_Captivity.htm.

5. Andrew Carnegie, Teamwork Quotes, Thinkexist.com, http://en.thinkexist.com/quotation/teamwork_is_the_ability_to_work_together_toward_a/256948.html.

6. Wikipedia, "John Wesley," http://en.wikipedia.org/wiki/John_Wesley.

7. Howard Snyder, *The Radical Wesley*, (Downers Grove: IVP, 1980), 26.

8. Victor Shepherd, "John Wesley: A Portrait," Sermons and Writings of Victor Shepherd, http://www.victorshepherd. on.ca/Wesley/newpage35.htm.

9. *Christianity Today*, 131 Christians Everyone Should Know, "John Wesley", http://christianitytoday.com/holidays/ fourthofjuly/features/Wesley.html.

10. Howard Snyder, *The Radical Wesley*, (Downers Grove: IVP, 1980), 63.

11. *Christianity Today*, 131 Christians Everyone Should Know, "John Wesley", http://christianitytoday.com/holidays/ fourthofjuly/features/Wesley.html.

Chapter 2: The Power of Agreement—Covenant

1. Roy Campbell, "Sir William Wallace," Significant and Famous Scots, Electricscotland.com, http://www. electricscotland.com/history/wallace.htm.

2. Tartans.com, "Sir William Wallace," Famous Scots, Resources, Tartans.com, http://www.tartans.com/modules. php.srl.op+modload,name+News,file+article,sid+114,mode +thread,order+0,thold+0.html.

3. The Biography Channel, "William Wallace," Biographies, The Biography Channel, http://www.thebiographychannel. co.uk/biography_story/860:0/1/William_Wallace.htm.

4. Clan McAlister of America, "William Wallace," Clan McAlister of America, http://www.clanmcalister.org/ wallace.html.

5. The Biography Channel, "William Wallace," Biographies, The Biography Channel, http://www.thebiographychannel. co.uk/biography_story/860:0/1/William_Wallace.htm.

6. "Are You Ready for War," *Braveheart*, DVD, Directed by Mel Gibson (Hollywood, CA: Paramount Pictures, 1995).

Chapter 3: O Brother, Where Art Thou?—Friendship

1. Chris Armstrong, "J.R.R. Tolkien and C.S. Lewis, A legendary Friendship," Christian History Corner, *Christianity Today*, August 29, 2003, http://www. christianitytoday.com/ct/2003/134/52.0.html.
2. Reverend Ed Hird, "Friends on a Quest," Spiritually Speaking, North Shore News, http://www3.telus.net/st_ simons/nsnews007.htm.
3. John Adcox, "Can Fantasy Be Myth? Mythopoeia and The Lord of the Rings, Mythic Passages, September/ October 2003, http://www.mythicjourneys.org/passages/ septoct2003/newsletterp8.html.
4. Don W. King, "Enchanted," Books and Culture, *Christianity Today*, January/February 2006, http://www. christianitytoday.com/bc/2006/001/4.18.html.
5. Chris Armstrong, "J.R.R. Tolkien and C.S. Lewis, A legendary Friendship," Christian History Corner, *Christianity Today*, August 29, 2003, http://www. christianitytoday.com/ct/2003/134/52.0.html.
6. *The Book of Positive Quotations*, Compiled by John Cook, (New York: Random House, Gramercy Books, 1999), 108.

Chapter 4: Life in a Cave—Brokenness

1. Wikipedia, "Watchman Nee," http://en.wikipedia. org/wiki/Watchman_Nee.
2. Contending for the Faith, Introduction, http://www. contendingforthefaith.org/index.html.
3. Rit Nosotro, "Watchman Nee," Hyperhistory.net, http://www. hyperhistory.net/apwh/bios/b3watchmannee_p2kk.htm.
4. Voidspace, "Imprisonment," Watchman Nee, Voidspace, http://www.voidspace.org.uk/spiritual/watchman_nee. shtml#imprisonment.

5. Wikipedia, "Watchman Nee," http://en.wikipedia.org/wiki/Watchman_Nee.
6. Voidspace, *Release of the Spirit*, Watchman Nee, Voidspace, http://www.voidspace.org.uk/spiritual/nee/rs01.htm.

Chapter 6: Following the King—Passionate Purpose
1. Don Milam, *The Lost Passions of Jesus,* (Shippensburg: Mercy Place, 1999).
2. Michal Ann Goll, W*omen on the Front Line,* (Destiny Image, 1999). Used by permission.
3. Ibid.
4. Ibid.

Chapter 7: Possessing Your Territory—Determination
1. Lucidcafe, "Martin Luther King, Jr., Civil Rights Leader," Biographies Archives, Lucidcafe, http://www.lucidcafe.com/lucidcafe/library/96jandking.html.
2. *Quotationary*, Leonard Roy Frank, (New York: Random House, 1999, 2001), 16.
3. Ibid., 663.
4. Ibid., 727.
5. Ibid., 690.

Chapter 8: Building a Dynasty—Unity
1. Vince Lombardi, Quoteworld.org, http://www.quoteworld.org/quotes/8407.
2. Agnes Savill, *Alexander the Great and His Time*, (New York: Barnes and Noble, 1993), 6.
3. Ibid., 5.
4. Ibid., 118-119.

About the
Author

ICK HAWKINS IS SENIOR PASTOR of the Family Praise Center in San Antonio, Texas, which he founded with his wife, Robin, in 1993. Family Praise Center is dedicated to sharing the uncompromised love and message of Jesus Christ, which is reflected in the integrated, multicultural, growing congregation of over 4,500 members.

"The physical, spiritual, and cultural landscape of a city, state, and nation should be imprinted with the influence of the body of Christ," insists Rick Hawkins. San Antonio is marked with his ministry philosophy. Pastor Rick and Robin are founders of The School of Excellence in Education, a public charter school in San Antonio, and The Nehemiah Institute, established to educate at-risk students who have been rejected by the public school system. Pastor Rick functions in the role of bishop in the covering of a select group of local and international churches and ministries, including several satellite churches and the Apostolic Training Center, an institution for leadership training. He was the first non-African American to receive San Antonio's Black Achievement Award for excellence in ministry and society.

In pursuing his passion for impact, Pastor Rick established a ministerial network, which includes in its circle of influence members throughout the nation and around the world. Recently Rick combined two of his life's greatest passions, ministry and team roping, in an outreach to the great American cowboy in arenas and rodeos throughout the nation.

Rick Hawkins is an international speaker and author of numerous books, tapes, and teaching series. Rick lives on a working ranch near San Antonio with his best friend and wife of thirty years, Robin. They have three children and three grandchildren.

MINISTRY INFORMATION

For more information on Family Praise Center,
Rick Hawkins, or to obtain additional teaching series,
books, and music, please visit our Web site at:

www.fpc.us

Or by mail:

Family Praise Center
5820 NW Loop 410
San Antonio, TX 78238

THE BENJAMIN BLESSING—
GOD'S FIVE-FOLD PLAN FOR YOUR DESTINY!
ISBN 1-932007-00-8

As you look with new clarity and under-
standing through the eyes of the Holy
Spirit—you will realize that you are
called and equipped with everything
you need times five to battle and win!
You are a chosen generation—you are
a Benjamite! The Benjamin Blessing
will equip you for a special mission—to
go forth and carry out God's purpose
and plan for your life and the last-day
church.

JUST PLAYIN' AROUND
Studio Music CD
ISBN 1-932007-02-4

Guitar picking at its best! Dedicated and
inspired by his late father, Rick Hawkins
recorded Just Playin' Around *with*
his friends, including David Huff and
Jonathan Dubose. "My Dad used to pull out his guitar for me
and just play around. Life is fun and should be enjoyed. I hope
this music inspires you to do something you enjoy."